CW00662731

Yum Cha

Yum Cha

DIM SIMS & OTHER CHINESE DELIGHTS

ELLA-MEI WONG

illustrated by
Lorraine Hannay

ANGUS & ROBERTSON PUBLISHERS

To K. C.
chief dim sim taster

ANGUS & ROBERTSON PUBLISHERS
London • Sydney • Melbourne • Singapore • Manila

First published by Angus & Robertson Publishers, Australia, 1981

National Library of Australia
Cataloguing-in-publication data.

Wong, Ella-mei
Yum Cha

Includes index.
ISBN 0 207 14127 4

1. Cookery, Chinese. I. Title.

641.5951

Typeset in Hong Kong by Graphicraft Typesetters

Printed in Hong Kong

Contents

Introduction

Teahouses have traditionally been the centre of Chinese social life. Even today, Chinese businessmen often conduct their transactions in the teahouses, and every section of the business community has its favourite place. In older-style teahouses, drinking tea and eating food is a leisurely entertainment, shared with friends. Often in the old days the teahouse provided a refuge for an old man with his pet bird in a cage. The bird was trained to leave the cage and walk out on to the table to tell the fortune of the passer-by who chose from a container a strip of paper on which the 'fortune' was written. The old teahouses always provided a place set apart for the bird's cage to hang.

It is in the teahouses that the Chinese take *yum cha* — which is a traditional greeting literally meaning 'drink tea' (with me), but in fact describes a delicious lunchtime tradition — a feast, a smörgasbord on wheels. First come the *deem sum*, piping hot savoury-filled pastries of many kinds, steamed in little bamboo baskets. The bamboo steamers are loaded on to trolleys which are wheeled around the restaurant by the waitress. The guest may select whatever appeals. Each basket contains only two to four pieces of food, each small enough to be eaten in one or two mouthfuls at a leisurely pace, sipping tea in between. After the food is eaten, the baskets are stacked one on top of the other, and at the end of the meal the cost is calculated by the number of empty baskets left on the table. Next come the deep-fried titbits: the little spring rolls, the crisp *won tun*, the prawn balls and toasts, and the steamed buns and pastries. Savoury dishes, like chicken wings, spare ribs or meatballs come next, followed by something sweet, like a chestnut slice or *darn* (custard) tart. Later there are noodles, braised or in soup, usually eaten with small dishes of soy sauce chicken, roast duck or

barbecued pork. The meats are accompanied by a dip sauce — hoisin, lemon, plum or chilli. Fragrant tea is sipped throughout the meal, which has an unhurried, casual elegance.

I have had *yum cha* all over the world — in Honolulu, San Francisco, New York, London, Hong Kong. Wherever there is a Chinese community the tradition is to be found, and each community has its own preferences and specialities. In this book I have given recipes for some of these most delicious and unusual Chinese delicacies. Most are not hard to make and many may be made beforehand and reheated. Here you will find superb *hors d'oeuvres*, first courses, luncheon dishes and dinners — and exotic breakfasts, if you're in the mood — not forgetting the intriguing Chinese sweetmeats, the festival cakes and dumplings, the desserts and the sweet pastries that make such magnificent afternoon teas.

Perhaps, now, you would like to put all these good things together and enjoy, as the Chinese do, a real *deem sum* lunch, your own *yum cha*.

Choose a few dishes from the four main categories: steamed things, deep-fried things, savoury things and sweet things — perhaps with some pastries and steamed buns for variety of texture and flavour. The noodle dish which usually follows can be replaced, if you like, by fried rice with savoury titbits, or something like the glutinous rice and chicken dish, steamed and served in individual basins. Towards the end of the book I have included some good dessert dishes suited to rounding off a *deem sum* lunch.

You will also find four menus which are just a guide to a good balanced meal; obviously the combinations are endless.

Chinese tea is served all through *yum cha*, but chilled white wine is also a good accompaniment.

Good eating!

Deem Sum and Gow Jees

Over a thousand years ago, during the Sung Dynasty, *deem sum* and *gow jees* became popular. Later, in the Ching Dynasty, the Cantonese became renowned for the finest and most delicate kinds of these appetisers.

The translation of *deem sum* is 'pointing to the heart', and *gow jee* means 'biting pieces of titbits'. What a perfect combination for *yum cha*! Dim sims, those exquisite appetisers, are designed to be enjoyed whenever the heart desires, and are not only delicious but are pleasing to the eye. They are small but satisfying, and consist of savoury meats, seasoned pork, seafood, vegetables, sweet purees and nuts wrapped in pastry. They are usually steamed in bamboo baskets (see Steamed Things, p. 1) and are often dipped in various sauces to heighten the flavour. (The Cantonese find steaming more acceptable because of the hot weather in the southern province.)

In the past, this speciality of Chinese cuisine was a closely guarded secret which was handed down from the head chef to his apprentice who took many years to master the different techniques. Nimble fingers are essential to shape and mould the dough, and an understanding of the texture of the pastry is also required — some of the pastry being almost transparent. In this technological age the pastry is made and shaped by machine, and the finished product can be purchased in fresh or frozen packs ready to be used at home. Other allied products such as the skins used in making spring rolls, wheat and rice flour noodles, and yeast dough are also made by machine, but they still manage to retain that refined taste reminiscent of ancient times. I have given recipes for the pastries used in the different types of *deem sum* but if you prefer to buy your pastry ready-made, be assured that the commercial product will give you a professional result.

You will find it astonishingly simple and satisfying to make the *deem sum* yourself. It is a good idea to make a large batch of each type and freeze them until required. Frozen *deem sum* are admirably suited to steaming and come up tasting and looking freshly made.

The Chinese Lunar Calendar

The Chinese lunar calendar divides the year into twelve months of twenty-nine or thirty days. Every thirty months, recorded time is adjusted to the movement of the moon by the addition of an extra month. The New Year is the first new moon after the sun enters the sign of Aquarius, which falls between 21 January and 19 February of the Gregorian (Western) calendar. However, time is officially recognised in terms of the Gregorian calendar, although the years are numbered from the founding of the Republic of China in 1911.

The Chinese zodiac has a cycle of twelve years instead of twelve months as in the Western world. Each year of the cycle has a particular animal symbol. One of the stories of how the Chinese astrological system began tells of how, on a certain New Year's Day, Buddha called on all the animals of the world to pay homage to him. In return they would receive a gift for their faithfulness and as a mark of honour would have a year named after them. Only twelve animals came, in this order: the rat and the ox; the tiger and the rabbit; the dragon and the snake; the horse and the ram; the monkey and the cock; the dog and the boar.

Each animal contributes its characteristic traits to an astrological year, and according to this belief, people born in a particular cycle will have those characteristic traits. It is from these twelve zodiac symbols that people may have their fortunes told. The symbols hold a mystical significance with regard to aspects of the human body, personality and character. The belief is that the symbols influence the sun and moon as well.

The order in which the animals appear in all cycles is always the same. To discover your animal year (according to this system 1900 was the year of the rat), count either forward or backward from 1900 to your birth year.

New Year

The first day of the first month in the Chinese lunar calendar, which is New Year's Day, heralds the most colourful and lavish of all the Chinese festivals. It is also one of the longest, and celebrations last as long as three weeks to a month. This is the time when food of all kinds is available and so New Year's Eve dinner is always lavish. There is a special New Year's dumpling made of glutinous rice, and as it is sweet, everyone is sure to eat a lot of it to ensure that the new year will be very sweet and happy. See recipe on page 61.

Lantern Festival

The New Year season ends on the fifteenth of the first month, when the first full moon of the year lights up the sky. This signals the commencement of the Lantern Festival. According to Buddhist belief, elaborate lanterns made in every conceivable shape and colour were used to look for celestial spirits flying about in the light of the first full moon. In rural villages this festival takes on the atmosphere of a street carnival. Stalls sell special sweets, and the special food for this occasion is the small round crisp dumpling made with glutinous rice flour and a sweet filling (see recipe on page 61). During the Lantern Festival there are puppet shows, fortune tellers and opera groups performing all night. The main attraction is the Dragon Dance. Lots of fireworks are displayed, and when the last flicker of the fireworks goes out, the New Year becomes just another lapse in the reckoning of time.

Dragon Boat Festival

The next important festival falls on the fifth day of the fifth moon. Its chief attraction is the Dragon Boat Race. Everyone makes the typical glutinous rice pudding with different fillings, and each pudding is individually wrapped in lotus leaves and steamed. The puddings are sent as gifts to friends and relatives and, as with all Chinese specialty food, a legend surrounds their origin. This one concerns a certain statesman of the Choo era (403 BC) who died a patriot by throwing himself into the Milo River in Hunan province when he realised he could not end corruption and conspiracy among the court officials. The people who respected this man for his honesty and integrity searched in boats for him in vain. Over time, legend developed these boats into dragon boats, and the race is held on the anniversary of his death. During the search for the patriot, the people threw rice into the river to appease his soul; but as soon as the rice was thrown into the river, the fish ate it, so the story goes, and the people hit upon the idea of wrapping the rice in leaves. The recipe for *Joong* or Dragon Festival pudding is on page 62.

Moon Festival

There is an old Chinese saying that 'to dream of moon cakes means lots of good luck and riches'. The Moon Festival falls on the fifteenth day of the eighth moon and the Chinese believe that only on this night is the moon at its fullest and brightest. *Yin*, or the female principle, which is personified by the moon in ascent at this time, makes it a female affair, and so, according to their religion, women worshippers pay their respects to the Moon Goddess. They light candles and burn incense and make offerings of food and fruit which are placed on an altar outside in the open.

This is the end of the harvest season, and if the crops are bountiful there is even more cause to celebrate. Harvest moon is a time for relaxation and for giving parties. As with every Chinese holiday, there is special food to accompany the festival. Appropriately, it is the moon cake. Weeks before the harvest moon the bakers start to make moon cakes and their appearance in the shops reminds everyone that the day draws near. These unique cakes are so popular that devotees usually buy them before the festival day with the result that they are sold out even before the Moon Festival begins. Moon cakes are packed four to a box or tin and are given away as gifts, so that most homes have at least four cakes during the festival.

One story about the origin of moon cakes goes back to the Yüan Dynasty (1368 AD) when the Chinese were plotting to overthrow their Mongol rulers. The Court confectioner conceived the brilliant idea of concealing secret messages inside cakes which were sent out as gifts, and in this way people were able to communicate with each other without being detected.

Most people will not attempt to make moon cakes at home because they believe the preparations are too difficult. Moon cakes are not hard to make, but valuable time is needed for their preparation. Special wooden moulds are needed and they must be custom made if you want a special design carved on the inside. Some of the designs people favour are family crests, flowers, birds or symbols of various kinds. The standard size of a moon cake is 8 cm (3 in) in diameter. The weight of the pastry and filling should not exceed 170 g (6 oz).

Fillings are varied and some have to be prepared weeks beforehand, unless, of course, they can be purchased locally. For instance, duck eggs have to be salted (see recipe on page 63); pork fat has to be cooked, cooled and left in sugar for two to three weeks before being added to other ingredients; rose petals have to be packed in sugar and allowed to mature at least nine months; pine melon and other fruits have to be crystallised. All this is done well before Moon Festival begins.

Learning the Secrets of the Chinese Kitchen

In early times the Chinese cooked their food over heated bricks, or buried in hot ashes and coal. Each community had a large oven made of heated rocks and bricks for all the people to use. As cookery methods progressed, they relied on twigs, dried branches or anything they could find to use as fuel. The people devised means of cooking that required the smallest degree of fire and caused the least possible amount of shrinkage to the food. They learned to adapt their methods so that food retained its goodness, for long experience had taught them the value of nutrition. Households, even the wealthy ones, used a series of clay pots and heated charcoal to cook their food. In those days, of course, manpower was cheap and willing, so that there were many *amahs* to prepare the fires for cooking.

Today we have an extraordinary range of cookery equipment from which to choose, using gas, electricity, and microwave ovens. Even so, as in the days of clay pots, one must master the techniques of cooking to ensure success in the kitchen.

Steamed Things

Steaming

Steaming is one of the easiest cooking methods to master, and since it is also most effective, it is one of the favourite ways of cooking in Chinese kitchens. There are two methods of steaming: direct and indirect.

Direct Steaming

This is also known as 'wet' steaming, as the steam comes into direct contact with the food. The best containers in which to 'wet' steam food are the traditional bamboo baskets. The industry of making these baskets is still thriving, despite the flow of modern steaming devices which appear so frequently on the market. This is a craft that is handed down from father to son and so the business of handmade bamboo baskets has always been a family affair. They are made in many sizes.

To use a bamboo basket, simply place the food inside on a heatproof plate for *jing* cooking, if the food is fish, chicken, spare ribs, meat balls or other meat; straight into the basket for *choy* cooking, if you are preparing steamed buns, dim sims or rice cakes. Cover the basket with the lid, and stand it in a saucepan or wok containing a little water. The food should not be in contact with the water. Bring the water to the boil. The food is cooked by the steam circulating around it. Be sure the pan does not boil dry.

If a bamboo basket is not available, substitute a heatproof dish standing on a wire stand or upturned bowl in the saucepan or wok. The water should come to about the base of the dish containing the food, but not so high that it will seep into the dish when boiling. Cover the saucepan or wok, bring the water to the boil and steam gently until the food is cooked.

Indirect Steaming

This method is used to steam foods that need a longer cooking time, such as large cuts of meat and steamed egg dishes. Place a bowl containing the food into a saucepan holding enough hot water to reach one-third to halfway up the sides of the bowl. Cover the saucepan with a tight lid and steam gently until food is cooked, checking now and then to ensure the water has not evaporated, and replenishing with hot water when necessary.

Steaming Food on Top of Rice

It is a good idea to use the steam rising from cooking rice to cook partly prepared foods or warm up other foods, and so have a complete meal in one pot. Place Chinese sausage, wax ducks (*larp arp*), dried pork (*larp yuk*), dried squid or salted fish in small dishes or saucers on top of the rice just at the stage when the water has evaporated. Replace the lid, and there will be sufficient steam to continue cooking the rice and to cook the food as well. (For a change, try adding hen or duck eggs to the rice just at the stage when the water starts to boil.)

Dim Sims

點心 (DEEM SUM)

250 g (8 oz) lean and fat pork, minced
125 g (4 oz) raw prawn meat, minced
8 dried mushrooms, soaked in warm water for 20 minutes and chopped finely
12 chopped fresh (or canned) water chestnuts (see p. 105)
1 egg white
1 teaspoon salt
¼ teaspoon white pepper
2 tablespoons rice wine (see p. 104)
1 teaspoon sesame oil
2 tablespoons peanut or vegetable oil
1 tablespoon cornflour
30 dim sim pastry rounds (p. 80)
a few chopped prawns
Soy sauce dip (see p. 87)

Combine pork mince, prawn mince, mushrooms and water chestnuts and mince to a paste. Mix in egg white, salt, pepper, rice wine, sesame oil, peanut or vegetable oil and cornflour. Stir well together, then knead lightly for 5 minutes.

Using a small flat wooden stick (such as an ice cream stick), chopsticks or a spoon place about 1 tablespoon of filling on the centre of each pastry round, taking care not to tear the pastry. Gather the pastry up to enclose this filling in a 'pouch'. Press edges together, leaving a little filling showing at the top. Place a small piece of prawn in this space. Press base on to a flat surface to allow the dim sim to stand up. Place in lightly greased bamboo or other kind of steamer and steam for 15 minutes. Serve with Soy sauce dip, as well as a chilli sauce, if liked.

Makes 30 dim sims.

Miniature dim sims

細點心 (SAI DEEM SUM)

250 g (8 oz) pork mince
125 g (4 oz) raw prawn meat, minced
4 dried mushrooms, soaked in warm water for 20 minutes, and chopped finely
1 shallot, chopped finely
1 tablespoon soy sauce
½ teaspoon salt
½ teaspoon sesame oil
1 beaten egg
30 dim sim pastry skins 5 cm (2 in) in diameter (p. 80)
few chopped prawns (optional)

Combine minced pork and prawn meat, mushrooms and shallots together in a small bowl. Mix in the soy sauce, salt and sesame oil, and stir in the beaten egg so that the mixture is like a thick paste.

Place 1 heaped teaspoon of mixture in centre of each pastry round and gather pastry around the filling, pressing together but leaving top of filling showing. Place a small piece of prawn in this space if desired. Lightly grease steamer or bamboo basket and arrange dim sims upright in it, close together. Steam for 20 minutes.

Serve with soy sauce, mustard or chilli sauce.

Makes 30 dim sims.

Prawn dumplings 1

蝦餃 (HAR GOW)

500 g (1 lb) raw prawns
1 small can bamboo shoots
½ cup peanut oil
white ends of 8 shallots, chopped
½ cup minced ham fat
30 *har gow* pastry rounds (p. 81)

Wash, peel and de-vein the prawns, then dice. Drain the liquid from the bamboo shoots, then cut into the same size dice. Heat wok or frying pan, add oil and sauté the prawns until they turn pink. Add the bamboo shoots and shallots, and cook for a further 1 minute. Allow mixture to cool, then mix in ham fat to set the mixture.

Make five small pleats on one side of each pastry round and fill with 1 tablespoon of mixture. Close edges by pressing together to form a pouch. Place in a lightly greased bamboo steamer, cover with lid and steam for 15 minutes.

Makes 30 dumplings.

Note This is the authentic recipe, but water chestnuts, mushrooms or barbecued pork, mixed with cooked prawns, may be used instead. Remember to chop the ingredients very finely and press tightly together before placing on the pastry.

Prawn dumplings 2

蝦餃 (HAR GOW)

500 g (1 lb) raw prawns
1 cup canned bamboo shoots, diced
1 tablespoon thin soy sauce
½ teaspoon salt
½ teaspoon sesame oil
1 tablespoon minced green ginger (see p. 100)
24 *fun gor* skins (p. 82)
vegetable oil

Wash, peel, de-vein and chop prawns. Combine with bamboo shoots, soy sauce, salt, sesame oil and ginger.

Place 2 teaspoons of filling on each pastry skin and close up the edges as described on p. 6. Arrange dumplings close together in lightly greased steamer or bamboo basket and brush them with a little vegetable oil to prevent the skin from drying out and to give a glossy finish. Steam for 15 minutes.

Serve with soy sauce or chilli sauce.

Makes 24 dumplings.

Meat balls with sheet bean curd

牛肉腐竹 (KNO YUK FOO JUK)

2-3 sheets of dried bean curd (see p. 97)
250 g (8 oz) beef, finely minced
½ cup finely chopped shallots
2 tablespoons chopped coriander leaves
1 beaten egg
salt and pepper

Soak the dried bean curd for 20 minutes in hot water and cut into 6 cm (2½ in) squares.

Combine the minced beef, shallots and coriander leaves together in a bowl. Mix in the beaten egg and season with salt and pepper. Knead together gently with the hands. Shape into small balls about 2.5 cm (1 in) in diameter.

Line 10 soy sauce dishes or small saucers with a sheet of bean curd and place 2 meat balls on top of each. Steam in a bamboo basket or other steamer for 15 minutes.

Serve immediately.

Makes 10 servings.

Transparent pastry savouries

(FUN GOR)

8 dried mushrooms, soaked in warm water for 20 minutes
150 g (5 oz) raw prawns
1 cup bamboo shoots, diced
¼ cup vegetable oil
150 g (4 oz) barbecued pork (p. 86), diced
2 tablespoons oyster sauce (see p. 102)
1 teaspoon sugar
1 teaspoon sesame oil
½ teaspoon salt
¼ cup stock (p. 28)
1 tablespoon cornflour
2 egg yolks
¼ cup toasted olive nuts
25 *fun gor* skins (p. 82)

Dice mushrooms, and peel, de-vein and dice prawns, then sauté mushrooms and prawns with bamboo shoots in hot oil for 3 minutes. Add pork and heat through. Stir in oyster sauce, sugar, sesame oil and salt and cook further for 1 minute. Pour in stock blended with cornflour and cook for another minute.

Remove from heat and stir in beaten egg yolks. Mix in the toasted olive nuts. Allow mixture to cool and set.

Divide mixture into 25 portions and roll into small balls. Place one portion on each pastry skin and close up. Pinch edges together to form a ruched pouch. Place in a lightly greased bamboo basket or other kind of steamer and steam for 15 minutes.

Makes 25 fun gor.

Pork and prawn filled pastries

 (SHUI MEI)

150 g (5 oz) pork mince
125 g (4 oz) raw prawn meat, minced
½ cup minced pork fat
½ cup diced, cooked bamboo shoots (fresh or canned)
1 egg white
1 tablespoon rice wine (see p. 104)
1 teaspoon salt
½ teaspoon white pepper
30 pieces *shui mei* pastry (p. 80)
1 egg yolk
1 tablespoon cornflour

Combine pork, prawn and pork fat minces and bamboo shoots. Mix together until almost a paste. Mix in the egg white and rice wine, then season with salt and pepper. Knead mixture so that it is moist and well blended.

Using a small flat wooden stick (such as an ice cream stick), chopsticks or a spoon, spread about 1 tablespoon of the filling into each pastry round, taking care not to tear the pastry. Then gather pastry together and squeeze, but do not completely close the top. Press base on flat surface so that the *shui mei* can stand up.

Mix egg yolk and cornflour together until firm. Using the round end of a chopstick, dot the top of the *shui mei* with the mixture. Place the *shui mei* in a lightly greased bamboo steamer and cook for 10 minutes.

Makes 30 shui mei.

Taro tart

芋頭糕 (WU TOW GO)

1 kg (2 lb) taro root
2 tablespoons vegetable oil
2 cups water
2 Chinese sausages, steamed and diced (see p. 99)
8 dried mushrooms, soaked in warm water for 20 minutes
2 slices smoked ham, diced
¼ cup dried shrimps, washed
4 shallots, chopped
2 cups plain flour
2 tablespoons cornflour
1 teaspoon salt
¼ cup vegetable oil
2¼ cups cool water
coriander leaves

Peel taro root, cut into rings, then into small dice. Heat wok or frying pan, add oil, and when hot sauté taro root until golden brown. Pour in water, cover and simmer until taro is soft, about 15 minutes. Pour off any excess liquid.

Dice mushrooms, and to the taro add mushrooms, Chinese sausage, smoked ham, shrimps and shallots, mixing well together.

Blend together the flour, cornflour, salt, vegetable oil and water to make a smooth batter. Add this batter to the taro mixture and mix well. Pour mixture into a greased Swiss roll tin. Place tin on stand in baking dish containing a little water. Cover all with aluminium foil, bring water to boil and reduce heat so that tart steams gently. Steam for 20 to 25 minutes, replenishing water when necessary.

Remove tin from baking dish, garnish top with coriander leaves and allow to cool. Cut into small wedges to serve.

Makes 15 to 20 slices.

Barbecued pork buns

叉燒包 (CHAR SIEU BAO)

250 g (8 oz) barbecued pork, (see p. 86), diced
2 or 3 shallots, cut in short lengths
1 tablespoon brown bean paste (see p. 98)
1 tablespoon oyster sauce (see p. 102)
1 teaspoon sugar
2 tablespoons vegetable oil
1½ tablespoons cornflour
¼ cup cool water
1 teaspoon sesame oil
16 rounds Basic steamed bread dough (p. 84)
16 squares greaseproof paper

Mix barbecued pork, shallots, brown bean paste, oyster sauce and sugar together in a bowl.

Heat wok or large frying pan and add oil. When hot, sauté the pork mixture for 2 minutes. Blend cornflour with the water and stir into pork mixture. Cook for a further 1 minute. Add sesame oil. Allow to cool.

Roll out the bread dough rounds to a diameter of 10 cm (4 in). Place 1 heaped tablespoon of filling in each round. Bring all the edges together to close. Twist the top to seal completely. Place each bun on a square of greaseproof paper. Allow to stand for 10 minutes, then steam in a bamboo basket or other steamer for 15 minutes. Before removing buns, spray with cold water to glaze them. Serve hot or cold.

Makes 16 buns.

Chicken buns

鷄包 (GAI BAO)

6 dried mushrooms, soaked in warm water for 20 minutes
2 cooked chicken breasts, sliced
1 tablespoon oyster sauce (see p. 102)
1 tablespoon hoisin sauce (see p. 101)
¼ teaspoon five-spice powder (see p. 100)
2 or 3 shallots
2 tablespoons vegetable oil
½ cup stock
1½ tablespoons cornflour
½ teaspoon sesame oil
16 rounds Basic steamed bread dough (p. 84)
16 squares greaseproof paper

Slice mushrooms and combine with chicken, oyster sauce, hoisin sauce and five-spice powder in a bowl. Cut the shallots into short lengths and add to the chicken mixture.

Heat wok or frying pan, add oil and when hot sauté the chicken mixture for 3 minutes. Pour in the stock blended with cornflour and stir until the mixture begins to thicken. Add sesame oil. Cook for another 1 minute. Allow mixture to cool. Roll dough rounds out to 10 cm (4 in) diameter.

Place 1 heaped tablespoon of chicken mixture in each round. Bring all the edges together, and close and twist the top to seal completely. Place each bun on a square of greaseproof paper. Allow to stand for 10 minutes, then steam in a bamboo basket or other steamer for 15 minutes. Before removing buns, spray with cold water to glaze them. Serve hot or cold.

Makes 16 buns.

Chicken and mushroom buns

冬菇鷄包 (DOONG GWOO GAI BAO)

Dough

6 cups plain flour
2 tablespoons baking powder
½ cup castor sugar
2 tablespoons lard or margarine
1½ cups warm water
24 squares greaseproof paper

Filling

500 g (1 lb) chicken meat, diced
2 tablespoons vegetable oil
8 dried mushrooms, soaked in warm water for 20 minutes
8 white ends of shallots, chopped
1 tablespoon soy sauce
½ teaspoon salt
1 tablespoon oyster sauce (see p. 102)
2 tablespoons rosé, rice wine (see p. 104) or sherry
1 teaspoon sesame oil
2 tablespoons cornflour
½ cup chicken stock

Sift flour and baking powder into a bowl and mix in the sugar. Work in the lard or margarine and form into a dough with the warm water. (The amount of water required will vary with different flours, so if too dry, add a little more water.) Knead the dough until smooth.

Fry the chicken meat in vegetable oil until it changes colour. Dice mushrooms, and add these, plus shallots, to chicken meat. Cook for 2 minutes. Mix in soy sauce, salt, oyster sauce, wine or sherry and sesame oil. Blend cornflour with chicken stock and add to mixture. Allow to cook for 3 minutes. Remove to a bowl and allow to cool.

Divide the dough into 24 pieces, and flatten each piece into a round with the palm of the hand. Divide the filling into 24 portions and place a portion in the middle of each dough round. Pleat the edge of the dough to close it up, and twist the dough to secure the join.

Place each bun on a square of greaseproof paper and arrange in a bamboo basket or other steamer about 2 cm (¾ in) apart. Steam for 15 to 20 minutes. Before removing buns, spray with cold water to glaze them. Serve hot or cold.

Makes 24 buns.

Glutinous rice and chicken

鶏球飯 (GAI KO FARN)

3 cups glutinous rice, soaked overnight
3 cups water
2 chicken breasts, sliced
1 tablespoon soy sauce
1 tablespoon oyster sauce (see p. 102)
1 teaspoon sesame oil
½ teaspoon salt
½ teaspoon sugar
2 tablespoons peanut oil
1 tablespoon brandy
6 dried mushrooms, soaked in warm water for 20 minutes
2 shallots

Pour off water from rice and place in a deep saucepan with 3 cups water. Bring to the boil, then turn down heat and simmer for 10 minutes. Spoon rice into 6 individual heatproof bowls.

Marinate chicken in soy sauce, oyster sauce, sesame oil, salt, sugar, peanut oil and brandy. Allow to stand 1 hour. During the last 10 minutes, add the mushrooms to the marinade.

Place some chicken and 1 mushroom on top of each bowl of rice, cover with a lid and steam for 20 minutes.

To serve, garnish with a length of shallot.

Serves 6.

Note The rice and chicken can also be wrapped in lotus leaves, tied up and boiled for 30 minutes.

Pork balls on bean curd

蒸豬肉腐竹 (JING JEE YUK FOO JOOK)

2 sticks dried bean curd (see p. 97)
1 cup beef stock
500 g (1 lb) lean pork
10 water chestnuts (see p. 105)
1 teaspoon salt
1 beaten egg
1 teaspoon sugar
1 teaspoon soy sauce
½ cup chopped white ends of shallots
1 tablespoon cornflour

Place bean curd in a bowl. Cover with hot water. Soak for 30 minutes. Drain and rinse, place in saucepan with stock and cook for about 20 minutes until tender. Drain and cool. When cool enough to handle, break bean curd up into 12 pieces. Put each on a small heatproof plate.

Mince pork and water chestnuts together into a bowl. Add salt, beaten egg, sugar, soy sauce and shallots. Mix well together and shape into small balls 2.5 cm (1 in) in diameter. Sprinkle very lightly with cornflour.

Place two pork balls on top of each piece of bean curd. Put plate in a bamboo basket or other steamer and steam for 20 minutes.

Makes 12 small individual servings.

Red dated kidneys

炒腰花 (HOONG JOH YEW)

1 small ox kidney
1 cup water
1 tablespoon salt
2.5 cm (1 in) green ginger, shredded (see p. 100)
¼ cup rice wine (see p. 104)
8 dried mushrooms, soaked in warm water for 20 minutes
20 red dates (see p. 104), soaked for 15 minutes
1 teaspoon washed black beans (see p. 97)
1 tablespoon peanut oil
1 teaspoon sesame oil
salt (optional)
sprig of coriander
steamed rice

Wash kidney, cut in half lengthwise and remove tissues, then cut into fine diagonal slices. Place in a bowl with water and salt and allow to stand for 10 minutes. Drain.

Mix in shredded ginger and rice wine. Allow to stand for 20 minutes. Slice the mushrooms, wash red dates thoroughly and remove the seeds if very large. (There is no need to remove the seeds if the dates are small.) Sprinkle sliced mushroom and red dates on top of kidney and mix in the black beans. Spoon over the peanut oil and sesame oil. Steam in a bamboo basket or other steamer for 20 minutes. During the steaming, turn the kidneys over in the bowl so that they cook evenly. Season with salt if desired (though the black beans should make the dish salty enough).

Garnish with coriander and serve with steamed rice.

Serves 4.

Mushroom cups

釀香菇 (YEUNG DOONG GWOO)

20 dried mushrooms
2 cups stock (p. 28)
2 tablespoons soy sauce
1 teaspoon sugar
1 teaspoon salt
¼ cup rice wine (see p. 104)
1 tablespoon cornflour
250 g (8 oz) raw prawn meat
10 white ends of shallots
3 large slices ham with fat
coriander leaves

Place cleaned mushrooms in a saucepan with stock, soy sauce, sugar, salt and rice wine. Simmer over low heat for 15 minutes. Remove mushrooms and drain, retaining liquid.

Cut off mushroom stems and arrange mushrooms upside down on a board. Sprinkle with a little cornflour.

Finely mince the prawns, shallots and ham, and fill each mushroom cap, making a peak with the mixture. Place the mushrooms in a flat heatproof dish and spoon 3 or 4 tablespoons of the mushroom liquid over them. Steam for 15 minutes.

Garnish with a coriander leaf on each peak. Serve hot or cold.

Makes 20 mushroom cups.

Deep-fried Things

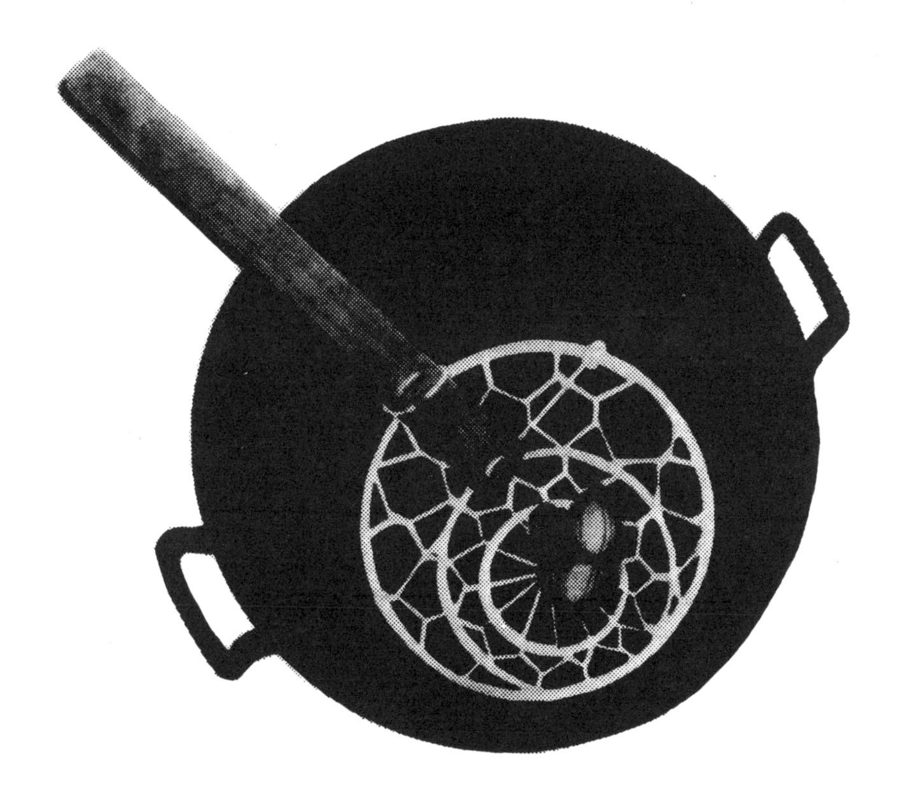

Deep-frying

Deep-frying is another popular Chinese cookery technique. Oil or fat, enough to completely cover the food to be cooked, is heated in a pan or wok. The temperature is very important to the success of deep-drying: if it is too low, the result is a soggy mess; if it is too high, the food will burn. Experiment by dropping a small crouton of bread into the oil. When it sizzles and rises to the surface, this will indicate that the oil temperature is correct for deep-frying small chunks of food coated with egg and breadcrumbs or batter. Lower the temperature a little for cooking larger pieces or whole fish or chicken. Remember that the temperature of the oil will drop if a lot of food is added to the pan at the same time, and make allowance for this.

Small items like dim sims should be placed in a wire scoop or strainer and then lowered into the oil to cook. (Always heat the wire scoop or strainer in hot oil first, otherwise the food will adhere to the utensil.) Even whole chicken, duck or fish can be cooked in a strainer, making it easy to lift out so that cooking progress can be checked. In Chinese cookery, whole birds and large cuts of meat are often deep-fried before being braised, to give them a glossy appearance.

Red-cooking

There are two ways of 'red cooking' — *hoong sui* and *loo sui*.

Hoong sui

In this process, literally meaning 'red roasting', the food is first deep-fried to brown the surface, then braised in stock and soy sauce.

Loo sui

This process is used to 'red cook' large cuts of pork, whole chickens, livers and gizzards. The food is marinated and cooked in a sauce consisting of a mixture of thin and thick soy sauces and a bag of mixed spices. The food takes on a rich colour and has an exceptionally delicate flavour. The marinade can be kept indefinitely for future use.

Beef balls in pastry

炸雲吞 (JOW WON TUN)

40 dim sim pastry skins (p. 80)
125 g (4 oz) minced beef
½ teaspoon salt
½ teaspoon soy sauce
1 small onion, minced
1 teaspoon brown beans (see p. 98), minced
1 beaten egg
4 cups vegetable oil for deep-frying
sweet and sour sauce (p. 88)
parsley for garnish

Place the minced beef in a bowl and mix in the salt, soy sauce, minced onion, minced brown beans and half the beaten egg. Heat wok or frying pan and add 1 tablespoon vegetable oil. When hot, sauté the beef mixture until it changes colour. Remove and allow to cool completely.

Put 1 heaped teaspoon of mixture in centre of 20 dim sim skins. Brush outer edge with remaining beaten egg and press another dim sim skin on top. Heat vegetable oil in a large saucepan and deep-fry the beef balls in moderately hot oil until golden brown. Drain on absorbent paper.

Garnish with parsley and serve with sweet and sour sauce, or as an hors-d'oeuvre.

Makes 20 beef balls.

Deep-fried dim sims

炸點心 (JOW DEEM SUM)

500 g (1 lb) minced beef
1 medium onion, finely chopped
½ teaspoon salt
¼ teaspoon curry powder
1 tablespoon soy sauce
1 teaspoon sesame oil
1 tablespoon vegetable oil
1 egg white
2 tablespoons finely chopped ham fat
25 dim sim pastry rounds (p. 80)
2 tablespoons cornflour
4 cups vegetable oil for deep-frying

Mix minced beef, onion, salt, curry powder, soy sauce, sesame oil, vegetable oil, egg white and ham fat in a large bowl.

Place 1 heaped tablespoon of mixture in centre of each dim sim skin and squeeze edges together firmly. Press base on a flat surface so that the dim sims will stand upright. Sprinkle the tops with a little cornflour.

Heat the vegetable oil in a wok or large saucepan. Using a strainer, deep-fry four or five dim sims at a time until golden brown. Keep turning them so that they cook evenly, adjusting the heat if necessary to prevent burning. Drain on absorbent paper.

Serve hot or cold with Soy sauce dip (p. 87) or chilli sauce.

Makes 25 dim sims.

Vegetarian dim sims

素菜點心 (CHING CHOY DEEM SUM)

2 stalks celery
¼ Chinese cabbage
1 cup bean sprouts
3 tablespoons peanut oil
½ cup finely sliced green beans
1 carrot, shredded
1 teaspoon salt
1 teaspoon sugar
1 teaspoon oyster sauce (see p. 102)
1 tablespoon cornflour, blended with a little water
25 dim sim pastry rounds (p. 80)
cornflour for dusting
1 beaten egg
4 cups vegetable oil for deep-frying

Peel and shred the celery, shred the Chinese cabbage, and blanch them together with the bean sprouts for 2 minutes. Retain the stock for use later in the recipe.

Heat peanut oil in wok or large frying pan. Fry the celery, Chinese cabbage, bean sprouts, beans and carrot for 2 minutes. Add salt, sugar and oyster sauce. Pour in ½ cup of the stock from the vegetables, stir in blended cornflour, and simmer for 3 minutes. Allow to cool.

Spoon a portion of the vegetable mixture on to each pastry round and close together tightly. Press base on flat surface so that the dim sims will stand up. Sprinkle top with a little cornflour and brush with beaten egg.

Heat oil in a wok or deep saucepan, and when hot, deep-fry the dim sims until golden brown. Drain on stale bread or absorbent paper.

Serve with Soy sauce dip (p. 87).

Makes 25 dim sims.

Fried gow jees

炸餃子 (JOW GOW JEES)

500 g (1 lb) pork, finely minced
1 teaspoon salt
1 tablespoon soy sauce
1 teaspoon sesame oil
1 tablespoon rice wine (see p. 104)
1 teaspoon sugar
1 tablespoon minced shallots
1 cup finely chopped cooked Chinese cabbage
24 pieces *gow jee* pastry (p. 81)
1 lightly beaten egg yolk
2 tablespoons vegetable oil
1 cup water

Combine the minced pork with the salt, soy sauce, sesame oil, rice wine and sugar and allow to marinate for 20 minutes. Mix in the shallots and Chinese cabbage.

Spread filling down the middle of each pastry round. Pleat one side of each pastry round, brush with beaten egg yolk, and press both edges together firmly.

Heat the oil in a frying pan, place *gow jees* in close together and fry until the bottoms are slightly browned. Pour in water, cover with a lid and cook over a moderate heat until no liquid is left.

To serve, remove lid, place serving plate over the *gow jee* and turn them out so that the brown sides face upwards. Soy sauce, mustard or chilli sauce may be placed on the table as an accompaniment.

Makes 24 gow jees.

Gourmet spring rolls

八寶春卷 (DUK BIT CHOON GUERN)

250 g (8 oz) barbecued pork (p. 86), cut into matchstick lengths
1 small can crab meat
10 dried mushrooms, soaked in warm water for 20 minutes
1 tablespoon peanut oil
½ cup cooked (canned or fresh) bamboo shoots, cut into matchstick lengths
3 cups shredded Chinese cabbage
salt
½ cup stock
2 tablespoons glutinous rice flour (see p. 101)
10 large spring roll skins (p. 82)
1 beaten egg
4 cups vegetable oil for deep-frying

Mix pork with crab meat. Slice mushrooms. Heat wok or frying pan, and when hot add peanut oil and fry the mushrooms, bamboo shoots and cabbage for 3 minutes. Add the pork and crab mixture and salt to taste. Pour in the stock and allow to simmer for 2 minutes, then stir in glutinous rice flour and cook for 2 minutes, or until the mixture starts to thicken. Allow to cool.

Divide mixture into 10 portions. Place spring roll skins one at a time on a board and spoon one portion of filling along the edge of each one. Wrap rolls up tightly, sealing the edges with beaten egg.

Heat vegetable oil in wok or large saucepan, and when hot lower the spring rolls in with the aid of a large strainer or chip basket. Cook until golden brown all over. Drain on absorbent paper. Serve hot or cold.

Makes 10 large spring rolls.

Potato puffs

鹹水角 (HARM SUEY GOCK)

2 cups glutinous rice flour (see p. 101)
2 medium potatoes
⅓ cup plain flour
2 tablespoons hot water
¾ cup finely diced barbecued pork (p. 86)
¼ cup finely diced bamboo shoots
1 small onion, finely diced
¼ cup dried shrimps, soaked and halved (see p. 100)
6 dried mushrooms, soaked in warm water for 20 minutes, and finely diced
1 tablespoon finely diced preserved green vegetable (see p. 104)
¼ cup minced ham fat
4 cups vegetable oil for deep-frying

Sift glutinous rice flour into a deep bowl. Boil potatoes until soft, then mash and mix into the glutinous rice flour. Stir in the plain flour. Mix in the water and knead into a dry dough. Take small pieces of dough about the size of a large walnut and roll into balls. Shape into small shallow cups about 5 mm (¼ in) thick.

Mix other ingredients together thoroughly. Place 1 tablespoon of filling in each cup and close the edges together. If desired, crimp the edges into a half-moon shape. Heat oil in a wok or large saucepan and deep-fry the puffs for 2 minutes until they are a very light brown. Drain on absorbent paper.

Makes about 20 puffs.

Deep-fried crab claws

炸蟹拑 (JOW HI KIM)

8 frozen crab claws
½ teaspoon salt
500 g (1 lb) raw prawn meat
½ cup cornflour
3 beaten eggs
1 cup breadcrumbs
4 cups vegetable oil for deep-frying
lemon wedges
parsley

Defrost crab claws and, if large, chop lengthwise in half. Add salt to prawn meat and mince until fine. Knead lightly. Press prawn mince tightly on to meat section of crab claws. Sprinkle with cornflour, dip into beaten egg and then into bread-crumbs, and place on a plate. Put in refrigerator and allow to 'set'.

Heat oil in a wok or large saucepan until hot and deep-fry crab claws until golden brown, rotating during cooking. Drain on stale bread or absorbent paper. Garnish with lemon wedges and parsley.

Makes about 8 crab claws

Note Alaskan crab claws can be bought by weight and are most suitable for this recipe because they are of uniform size.

Bean curd rolls

腐竹卷 (TOFU GUEN)

250 g (8 oz) lean pork, finely diced
1 teaspoon soy sauce
½ teaspoon salt
¼ teaspoon pepper
½ teaspoon sesame oil
2 tablespoons vegetable oil
1 clove garlic, crushed
1 large onion, finely sliced
250 g (8 oz) raw prawns, peeled (retain shells for stock) and finely chopped
2 cakes bean curd, finely sliced
1 cup canned bamboo shoots, cut into matchsticks
½ cup prawn stock (see below)
24 spring roll skins (p. 82)
1 lightly beaten egg yolk
4 cups vegetable oil for deep-frying

Marinate the diced pork in soy sauce, salt, pepper and sesame oil for 15 minutes.

Heat wok or frying pan, add vegetable oil and sauté garlic and onion until transparent. Add pork and sauté for 5 minutes. Remove. Put in prawns and bean curd, and cook until prawns turn pink. Add bamboo shoots and prawn stock. Return pork mixture to pan and mix well together. Season to taste. Allow mixture to cool.

Divide mixture into 24 portions. Place each portion on a separate pastry skin and roll up tightly, sealing the edges well with a little egg yolk. Place in refrigerator for 1 hour.

Heat oil in a wok or deep saucepan and deep-fry rolls until golden brown. Drain on absorbent paper.

Makes 24 rolls.

Prawn stock
Place washed prawn shells and heads, ½ teaspoon salt and 1½ cups water in a saucepan. Bring to boil and simmer 5 minutes. Strain.

Chicken and ham roll (large)

鷄卷 (GAI GUEN)

1 whole chicken
1 teaspoon salt
1 tablespoon soy sauce
1 tablespoon vegetable oil
1 teaspoon five-spice powder (see p. 100)
3 or 4 lengths lean ham, 1.5 cm (½ in) square
6 sheets pork caul (see p. 102)
3 beaten eggs
¼ cup cornflour
4 cups vegetable oil for deep-frying

Starting from the back of the chicken, carefully cut away in one piece all the meat from the bone. Remove skin. Flatten the meat with a wooden mallet and sprinkle with salt, soy sauce, vegetable oil and five-spice powder. Roll up and let stand for 20 minutes. Unroll the chicken, place lengths of ham end to end on longest edge and roll up tightly. Wash the pork caul thoroughly, being careful not to tear it, as it is very delicate. Lay it on working surface, put the chicken roll on top of it and wrap the pork caul around the chicken. Pour the beaten eggs into a large flat dish and brush the roll all over with egg. Sprinkle with cornflour and place in refrigerator for 20 minutes to set the egg coating.

Heat the oil in a large wok or large deep frying pan and, when hot, slide in the chicken roll gently. Deep-fry until golden brown, ladling hot oil over it if not completely immersed. Drain on absorbent paper.

When cool, cut into small pieces.

Makes 15 to 20 pieces.

Chicken and ham rolls (small)

火腿鷄卷 (FAW TOH GAI GUEN)

2 chicken breasts
½ teaspoon soy sauce
½ teaspoon salt
8 thin, flat slices of ham fat
4 slices cooked ham, 1.5 cm (½ in) thick
2 beaten eggs
cornflour
3 cups vegetable oil for deep-frying
coriander or parsley

Remove skin and bone from chicken breasts and cut into four flat slices 1.5 cm (½ in) thick. Season with soy sauce and salt and allow to stand for 15 minutes. Place 1 or 2 slices of ham fat (enough to roll around chicken) on a board and flatten with the side of a cleaver. Put one slice of chicken and one slice of ham on to ham fat and roll up firmly, securing with a toothpick. Dip into beaten egg and then into cornflour.

Heat oil in wok or large saucepan and deep-fry the rolls until golden brown. Drain on absorbent paper.

Garnish with coriander or parsley.

Serves 4.

Chinese doughnuts

油條 (YOW JOW GWAH)

4 cups strong flour (or 3½ cups plain flour and ½ cup gluten)
1 small packet (1 tablespoon) dried yeast
½ cup hot water
1 teaspoon sugar
1 cup warm water
flour for dusting
4 cups vegetable oil for deep-frying

Sift the strong flour on to a large board and make a well in the centre. Dissolve yeast in hot water and add sugar. Allow to stand for 10 minutes. Pour yeast mixture into the flour and make a dough with the warm water. Knead dough for 5 minutes, then put it into a lightly greased bowl, cover with a cloth and allow to stand in a warm part of the kitchen for 40 minutes or longer until the dough at least doubles in bulk.

Dust a board with a little flour. Knead dough again lightly and roll out into a long flat strip 5 cm by 0.5 mm (2 by ¼ in), then cut it into strips 1 cm (½ in) wide. Group the strips in pairs, placing one on top of the other. Press the centres with a rolling pin to make them more secure.

Heat oil in wok or frying pan ready for deep-frying. Pick up a paired strip of dough and stretch as long as possible (approximately 40 cm/15 in). Place in hot oil and using ladle make both ends meet so that the dough is divided in half, and will join together while cooking, as the dough expands. Deep-fry until golden brown. Drain on absorbent paper.

Makes about 12 doughnuts.

Red yam puffs

芋角 (WU GOCK)

Pastry

454 g (1 lb) packet red yam flour
½ cup Chinese wheat starch (see p. 106)
¼ cup lard
½ cup warm water

Filling

2 tablespoons vegetable oil
250 g (8 oz) pork mince
150 g (5 oz) raw prawn meat, diced
100 g (4 oz) barbecued pork (p. 86), diced
1 cup stock
2 tablespoons cornflour, blended with a little water
1 tablespoon oyster sauce (see p. 102)
1 tablespoon hoisin sauce (see p. 101)
4 cups vegetable oil for deep-frying

Empty red yam flour on to a board and mix in the wheat starch. Make a well in the centre and put in softened lard and water. Knead into a soft dough, then divide into 20 pieces.

Heat wok or frying pan, and when hot add oil and fry the pork mince until it changes colour. Leave on one side of wok, add a little more oil if necessary and fry the diced prawns until they turn pink. Add the barbecued pork, mix all together thoroughly and cook a further 2 minutes. Pour in stock and blended cornflour. Add oyster sauce and hoisin sauce. Cover and simmer for 5 minutes. Allow to cool.

Divide into 20 portions. Flatten each portion of pastry on to palm of hand and work it into an oval shape. Place filling in the centre and close securely, making an oval-shaped puff.

Heat vegetable oil in a wok or large saucepan and deep-fry at moderate heat until the outside is crisp. Drain on absorbent paper.

Makes 20 puffs.

Diced bread prawn balls

炸蝦仁 (JOW HAR YIN)

500 g (1 lb) raw prawn meat
12 white ends of shallots
salt and pepper
½ cup minced ham fat
1 beaten egg
8 slices stale white bread
3 eggs
2 teaspoons soy sauce
4 cups vegetable oil for deep-frying

Finely mince the prawns and shallots together. Season with salt and pepper. Stir in the ham fat and 1 beaten egg. Knead gently to combine ingredients. Shape into balls 4 cm (1½ in) in diameter.

Cut stale bread into small dice. Beat together the three eggs and soy sauce. Roll the prawn balls in the egg and soy sauce mixture and press diced bread on to them. Place in the refrigerator for 20 minutes to 'set'.

Heat oil in a wok or large saucepan. When sizzling hot, place the pork balls in to brown the diced bread. Turn the heat down immediately and cook for 5 more minutes to ensure that the prawn balls are cooked through. Drain on absorbent paper.

Makes about 25 prawn balls.

Prawn sticks

蝦麵包條 (HAR TU MIN BAO)

250 g (8 oz) raw prawn meat
1 teaspoon thin soy sauce
1 teaspoon sesame oil
½ teaspoon salt
1 egg
2 tablespoons chopped coriander leaves
6 slices stale white bread
3 cups vegetable oil for deep-frying

Mince prawn meat to a fine paste, then stir in the soy sauce, sesame oil and salt. Mix in the egg and coriander leaves. Cut the bread into thin strips and spread the prawn mixture evenly on one side.

Heat oil in wok or saucepan until very hot. Holding the prawn stick prawn side downwards with chopsticks or tongs, deep-fry until golden, then turn over and deep-fry the other side. Drain on stale bread or absorbent paper.

Makes about 30 sticks.

Note Prawn sticks can be re-heated in a very slow oven if they have been made beforehand.

Prawn toast

蝦多士 (HAR MIN BAO)

250 g (8 oz) raw prawn meat, minced
6 fresh water chestnuts (see p. 105), minced
1 egg white
½ teaspoon salt
7 slices stale bread
1 slice lean ham
4 cups vegetable oil for deep-frying

Mix together minced prawns with water chestnuts, egg white and salt. Cut bread into fancy shapes or, if you prefer, simply cut each slice into four pieces. Spread prawn mixture liberally over one side of bread and press small lengths of ham in the centre.

Heat oil in a wok or large saucepan until hot. Holding the bread with chopsticks or tongs, prawn side down, deep-fry until golden. Then turn over and cook the other side a few seconds longer. Drain on stale bread or absorbent paper.

Makes about 30 pieces.

Savoury Things

Wrapped lettuce

生菜包 (SARNG CHOY BAO)

1 lettuce
3 chicken breasts
4-6 chicken livers
100 g (4 oz) lean pork
1 egg yolk
2 tablespoons rice wine (see p. 104)
½ teaspoon salt
1 tablespoon rice flour
12 water chestnuts (see p. 105)
8 dried mushrooms, soaked in warm water for 20 minutes
2 tablespoons vegetable oil
½ cup chicken stock
1 tablespoon soy sauce
1 teaspoon sesame oil
1 cup vegetable oil
60 g (2 oz) cellophane noodles

Wash lettuce leaves thoroughly and place in a bowl of cold water to crisp. Pat dry. Place leaves on top of each other and cut them into the shape of a deep round cup. Invert over a small saucer.

Mince the chicken breasts, chicken livers and pork together finely and place in a bowl. Mix in the egg yolk, rice wine, salt and rice flour. Chop the water chestnuts and mushrooms into a coarse mince and stir into the chicken mixture.

Heat wok or large frying pan and when hot add the 2 tablespoons of vegetable oil. Fry the chicken mixture for 5 minutes. Pour in stock, soy sauce and sesame oil. Cover and simmer for 5 minutes. Remove and place on a warm platter.

Clean wok or frying pan and heat the 1 cup of vegetable oil. Deep-fry cellophane noodles until they are a white mass, which will take about half a minute. Drain on absorbent paper. Place the noodles around the chicken filling and crush gently.

To serve, spoon the chicken filling and noodles into lettuce cups and fold tops of cups around to close. Eat with the fingers.

Serves 6.

Chicken wings in soy sauce

抽王鷄翼 (SEE YO GAI YICK)

12 chicken wings
¼ cup thin soy sauce
2 tablespoons hoisin sauce (see p. 101)
¼ cup rice wine (see p. 104)
½ cup vegetable oil
1 tablespoon sesame oil
1 tablespoon sartee sauce (see p. 87)
1 teaspoon salt
2.5 cm (1 in) green ginger, crushed (see p. 100)
1 clove garlic, crushed

Cut chicken wings into three sections. Mix all ingredients together and marinate for 1 hour, turning chicken wings occasionally.

Cover a wire rack with aluminium foil and place on a baking tray. Put the chicken wings on the wire rack and cook in hot oven for 5 minutes until brown and crisp, then turn down heat to moderate, and cook a further 10 minutes or until done. Brush with marinade while cooking.

Serves about 12 people as an hors d'oeuvre.

Braised chicken wings

炆鷄翼 (MUN GAI YICK)

10 chicken wings
1 tablespoon thin soy sauce
½ teaspoon salt
3 cups vegetable oil
2 cloves garlic, minced
2 tablespoons oyster sauce (see p. 102)
1 cup chicken stock
1 tablespoon cornflour, blended with a little water
½ teaspoon sesame oil

Cut the chicken wings into two sections and season with the soy sauce and salt. Heat oil in a wok or frying pan and deep-fry the chicken wings until golden brown. Remove and drain on absorbent paper.

Fry the garlic in a little oil until slightly browned and add the chicken wings, oyster sauce and chicken stock. Cover and simmer for 15 minutes.

Stir blended cornflour into mixture. Cook a further 1 minute. Mix in the sesame oil and correct seasoning.

Serve hot with steamed rice.

Serves 4.

Steak and onions Chinese-style

中式牛柳 (KNO YUK PAR)

1 whole fillet beef or oyster blade steak with all fat and sinews removed
2 tablespoons thin soy sauce
1 tablespoons oyster sauce (see p. 102)
1 tablespoon rice wine (see p. 104)
1 teaspoon sugar
1 teaspoon sesame oil
2 tablespoons peanut oil
½ teaspoon salt
2 tablespoons vegetable oil
2 large onions, cut into rings
250 g (8 oz) *shirataki* (very special with this recipe — see p. 105)
extra vegetable oil for frying

Slice meat finely across the fillet. (If using oyster blade steak, gently flatten with side of cleaver to tenderise.) Spread meat out on a flat tray. Mix together the soy sauce, oyster sauce, rice wine, sugar, sesame oil, peanut oil and salt. Pour over the meat and allow to marinate at least 30 minutes.

Heat wok or large frying pan and when hot add the 2 tablespoons vegetable oil and fry the onions until golden brown. Remove to a sizzling platter.

Cook *shirataki* in boiling water for 10 minutes. Drain. Mix with the onions on the hot platter.

Heat wok again and add extra vegetable oil. When hot, fry each piece of fillet separately on both sides until just seared or cooked according to preference.

To serve, arrange the beef on sizzling platter with fried onions and noodles.

Serves 4 to 6 (depending on size of fillet).

Curried beef turnovers

嘌喱牛丸 (GARLEE KNO YUK YIN)

Pastry

3 cups plain flour
½ teaspoon salt
1 cup shortening (butter, lard or margarine)
1 teaspoon sugar
¼ cup cool water

Filling

500 g (1 lb) minced round steak
¼ cup vegetable oil
1 large onion, finely chopped
2 cups finely chopped cabbage
1 teaspoon salt
2 teaspoons sugar
1 tablespoon curry powder
1 teaspoon soy sauce
1 beaten egg

Sift flour and salt into a bowl. Add sugar. Rub in the shortening, and add water gradually to make a pliable dough. (Or, if you have a blender, use it to mix the flour, shortening, sugar and salt together, and add water gradually until the mixture just holds together.) Turn out on to a board and knead gently. Make into two long rolls 2.5 cm (1 in) in diameter and cut each into 15 even lengths. Roll out into rounds 8 cm (3 in) in diameter.

Fry the minced steak in hot vegetable oil until it changes colour, then add the onion, cabbage and salt. Mix together thoroughly while cooking for 2 minutes. Add the sugar, curry powder and soy sauce and cook a further 1 minute. The liquid coming from the cabbage as it cooks will moisten the mixture slightly. Allow to cool.

Place 1 tablespoon of filling in the centre of each pastry round and seal the edges together with beaten egg. Flute the edges of the turnovers. Place on lightly greased tray, brush the tops with beaten egg and bake in a moderate oven for 15 to 20 minutes until golden brown.

Makes 30 turnovers.

Curry puffs

咖喱角 (GARLEE GOCK)

500 g (1 lb) minced beef, *or* mixture of pork and beef
1 large onion, diced
2 tablespoons vegetable oil
1 or 2 tablespoons curry powder, according to taste
1 large potato, grated
1 cup coconut milk (p. 88)
1 teaspoon salt
20-30 pastry rounds (see below)
1 beaten egg

Mix the minced beef with the onion. Heat wok or large frying pan, and when hot add oil. Fry the meat until it changes colour, add the curry powder and fry for a further 1 minute. Add the grated potato and coconut milk and stir continuously until the mixture thickens. Add salt to taste. The mixture should be slightly congealed, but not dry. Allow to cool.

Make up the pastry according to the recipe on page 39 and roll out 3 mm ($\frac{1}{8}$ in) thick. Cut into rounds 6 cm (2½ in) in diameter.

Spoon a little filling in the centre of each pastry round and seal the edges together with beaten egg or water. Brush the top of each puff with beaten egg.

Place on a lightly greased baking tray and bake in a moderate oven for about 15 to 20 minutes or until pastry is golden brown.

Makes 20 to 30 puffs.

Note These curry puffs can be made a little smaller and deep-fried until golden brown.

Cellophane curry

珍絲咪喱 (JUN SEE GARLEE)

500 g (1 lb) minced topside
2 cm (¾ in) green ginger, shredded (see p. 100)
½ cup vegetable oil
1 large onion, chopped
2 cloves garlic, crushed
2 small pickling onions, quartered
2 tablespoons curry powder
1 small carrot, shredded
½ cup beef stock
¾ cup cellophane noodles cut up into 1.5 cm (½ in) lengths
1 teaspoon salt
2 teaspoons sesame oil
shredded lettuce
coriander leaves
steamed rice

Soak cellophane noodles in warm water for 10 minutes.

Mix minced topside together with ginger in a bowl. Heat wok or frying pan, add half the vegetable oil and fry the chopped onion, garlic and small onions until transparent. Add curry powder and fry for a further 3 minutes until fragrant. Add the rest of the vegetable oil and allow to heat another minute. Add the minced topside and keep stirring until browned. (The mixture should be dry, as the beef will absorb the moisture.)

Add the shredded carrot, stock and cellophane noodles. Cover and simmer for 15 to 20 minutes. Just before serving add salt and sesame oil.

Garnish with shredded lettuce and coriander leaves and serve with steamed rice.

Serves 6.

Oyster sauce roast pork

蠔油叉燒 (HOR YO CHAR SIEU)

3 or 4 fillets of pork
4 tablespoons soy sauce
1 tablespoon castor sugar
2 tablespoons oyster sauce (see p. 102)
1 teaspoon salt
¼ cup rice wine (see p. 104)
2.5 cm (1 in) green ginger, crushed (see p. 100)
2 cloves garlic, crushed
1 teaspoon five-spice powder (see p. 100)
2 drops red food colouring

Mix all ingredients together and marinate pork fillets in a shallow bowl for 30 minutes, turning over occasionally.

Place pork fillets on a wire rack over a shallow tray with a little water in it and roast in a very hot oven for 10 minutes. Reduce heat to moderate and cook for a further 20 minutes. Turn fillets over once during cooking. The meat is done when the outside becomes glazed and reddish-brown in colour. Slice thinly and serve with fried rice.

Serves 8.

Braised spare ribs

辣椒排骨 (LART JU PYE GWUT)

500 g (1 lb) pork spare ribs
¼ cup peanut oil
2 cloves garlic, crushed
2.5 cm (1 in) green ginger, shredded (see p. 100)
3 tablespoons canned brown beans (see p. 98)
1 teaspoon sugar
½ cup beef stock
1 hot chilli, shredded
shallot flowers (see below)

Chop spare ribs into short lengths and remove any excess fat. Heat wok or frying pan, add peanut oil and brown garlic and ginger. Add spare ribs and sauté for 2 minutes. Blend in the brown beans, sugar and stock. Allow to come to the boil, then cover and simmer for 10 minutes. Mix in the chilli.

Serve hot, garnished with shallot flowers.

Serves 4.

Shallot flowers

Cut off roots and cut shallots into 5 cm (2 in) lengths. With a razor blade or small sharp knife, cut each piece 3-4 times from end, but be careful not to cut right through. Stand in a bowl of cool water. The longer they are allowed to stand, the curlier they will become.

Sweet and sour spare ribs

咕咾排骨 (GOO LOO PYE GWUT)

1 kg (2 lb) pork spare ribs
2 tablespoons thin soy sauce
¼ cup vegetable oil
1 teaspoon sesame oil
1 teaspoon salt
2 tablespoons *mirin* (see p. 102)
2 tablespoons hoisin sauce (see p. 101)
4 cups vegetable oil for deep-frying
1 small can pineapple pieces
1 tablespoon tomato sauce
1 teaspoon Worcestershire sauce
¼ cup white vinegar
2 tablespoons sugar
1 beef stock cube
1 small green cucumber, peeled, seeded and cut into small logs
4 hot red chillies, sliced
1 tablespoon cornflour, blended with a little water
coriander leaves *or* shallot flowers (p. 42)

Chop spare ribs into short lengths and steam for 10 minutes. Place in a deep bowl with soy sauce, ¼ cup vegetable oil, sesame oil, salt, *mirin* and hoisin sauce. Marinate for 30 minutes.

Heat 4 cups vegetable oil in wok or saucepan and deep-fry spare ribs until golden brown. Place on a platter and keep warm.

Place liquid from canned pineapple, tomato sauce, Worcestershire sauce, vinegar and sugar in a saucepan and bring to the boil. Simmer for 3 minutes. Crumble in the stock cube and stir until dissolved. Add pineapple pieces, cucumber and chillies and simmer a further 2 minutes. Stir in blended cornflour and cook until sauce thickens. Pour over the spare ribs.

Garnish with coriander leaves or shallot flowers. Serve with plain fried rice.

Serves 6.

Salted duck eggs

鹹蛋 (HARM DARN)

1.5 litres (2½ pints) water
1 cup rock salt
10 duck eggs
1 teaspoon vegetable oil

Bring water and salt to the boil. Allow to cool. Pour into an earthenware or china jar with a tightly fitting lid. Add the eggs and seal. Set aside in a cool place for 8 weeks.

When ready to use, put eggs in a saucepan, cover with cold water, bring to the boil and simmer for 15 minutes.

Cut each egg in half through the shell and spoon out on to a small saucer. Spoon warm vegetable oil over it and serve with plain steamed rice.

Note If using salted eggs for moon cakes (p. 63) or for Dragon Festival pudding (p. 62), remember that only the yolk is used. The whites may be steamed later with pork mince to make another dish.

Noodle Dishes

Egg, Wheat & Rice Noodles

There were times when noodles were made by hand, the dough being rolled to the desired thickness and then cut into lengths. A small round bamboo stick was used to separate the strands. The noodles were then conveyed to a large bamboo rack and hung out in the sun to dry. I know that there are some factories still using this method, but with the population explosion and the growing demand for noodles, this art of making noodles will surely soon become part of history. Although machine-made noodles do not taste the same as home-made ones, they have the advantage of being conveniently packaged and uniform in size.

Noodles are always served towards the end of a banquet, braised in a rich stock without trimmings other than a garnish of coriander or shallot. At lunch or as an evening snack they accompany savoury foods and are either served in soup or fried. There are many varieties, but the general rule is that rice noodles and fine egg noodles are either used in soup or are braised, and wheat noodles are fried.

The term 'long soup' refers to long thin wheat noodles, and 'short soup' means *won tun*. Thus 'long and short soup' consists of a mixture of both noodles served in a deep bowl of seasoned soup with a green vegetable and chopped shallots. A side dish of chicken, barbecued pork or duck accompanies the soup. It is a satisfying lunch. A larger version of *won tun* is *sui gow*, although it is wrapped differently and the pastry enclosing the pork mince filling is pleated on top. *Sui gow* is served in soup with lettuce and chopped shallots, accompanied by a soy sauce dip or chilli sauce.

Braised noodles

炆伊麵 (MUN EE MEIN)

250 g (8 oz) fresh noodles, *or* spaghetti *or* vermicelli
1 tablespoon sesame oil
2 tablespoons vegetable oil
½ bunch Chinese cabbage
2.5 cm (1 in) green ginger, grated (see p. 100)
1 clove garlic, crushed
1 teaspoon salt
1 tablespoon sugar
250 g (8 oz) diced mixed barbecued pork (p. 86) and cooked duck (p. 85)
½ cup chicken stock
1 tablespoon thin soy sauce
¼ cup chopped shallots

Place fresh noodles in a large saucepan of boiling water and cook for 5 minutes, stirring occasionally to loosen the noodles. Drain in colander and run cold water through to remove starchy taste and to prevent further cooking. If you are using spaghetti or vermicelli, cook according to instructions. Mix sesame oil through noodles.

Heat wok or large frying pan, and when hot add vegetable oil and fry the Chinese cabbage with the grated ginger, garlic, salt and sugar. Cook for 2 minutes. Remove to a platter, including any liquid remaining from the cabbage.

Place noodles in the wok or pan and heat through. Return the cabbage and liquid, add diced pork and duck, stock and soy sauce. Mix well together, cover and braise for 4 minutes. Correct seasoning.

To serve, sprinkle with chopped shallots. Delicious either hot or cold.

Serves 4.

Chicken chow mein

鷄球炒麵 (GAI CHOW MEIN)

250 g (8 oz) fresh egg noodles, bought or home-made (p. 83)
4 cups vegetable oil for deep-frying
10 dried mushrooms, soaked in warm water for 20 minutes
2 tablespoons vegetable oil
150 g (5 oz) chicken meat, shredded
100 g (3½ oz) cooked ham, shredded
10 water chestnuts (see p. 105), sliced
salt and pepper
1 cup fresh bean sprouts, blanched
½ cup chicken stock
1 teaspoon cornflour
1 tablespoon soy sauce
1 teaspoon oyster sauce (see p. 102)

Shake noodles to remove excess flour and divide into four portions. Heat 4 cups oil in wok or large saucepan and deep-fry each portion until golden brown. Drain on absorbent paper. Store in an airtight container.

Slice mushrooms. Heat wok or frying pan, add two tablespoons vegetable oil, and when hot fry the chicken until it changes colour, then add ham, water chestnuts, mushrooms, salt and pepper. Cook for 1 minute, then add the bean sprouts, stock, cornflour blended with the soy sauce, and oyster sauce. Mix well together and cook for a further 5 minutes. Adjust seasoning to taste.

Spread the noodles out on a platter, spoon the chicken filling on top and serve immediately.

Serves 4.

Note Extra soy sauce and chilli sauce may accompany the fried noodles.

Savoury noodle rolls

粉卷 (GUEN FUN)

500 g (1 lb) barbecued pork (p. 86), finely diced
1 cup cooked peeled prawns
2 slices cooked ham, diced
½ cup finely diced bamboo shoots
¼ cup diced shallots
¼ cup preserved salted cabbage (see p. 104)
10 dried mushrooms, soaked for 20 minutes in warm water
fun batter (p. 84)
coriander leaves

Mix the barbecued pork, prawns, ham, bamboo shoots, shallots and salted cabbage together in a bowl. Boil the mushrooms for 15 minutes, then dice and add to mixture in bowl.

Make the *fun* batter and pour a thin layer into a lightly greased cake tin. Spoon a layer of the mixture on top, sprinkle with chopped coriander leaves and steam for 3 or 4 minutes. Remove and allow to cool.

Loosen the edges with a knife and roll up. Serve noodle roll hot (re-steamed) or cold, cut up into sections.

Makes 10 to 12 rolls.

Note Any variety of cooked meat can be substituted for the pork. Chinese sausage is excellent (see p. 99). Dried shrimps can be used in place of the fresh prawns (they must be soaked for 1 hour).

Rice noodle rolls

沙河粉卷 (SAR HOR FUN GUERN)

12 dried mushrooms, soaked and boiled in stock for 15 minutes
2 cups diced cooked chicken
½ cup slivered shallots
coriander leaves
1 cup bean sprouts, blanched
500 g (1 lb) flat sheets of rice noodle pastry, bought or home-made (see *fun*, p. 84)
1 egg, made into an omelet and shredded

Slice mushrooms and mix them together with chicken, shallots, coriander leaves and bean sprouts.

Spread sheet of rice noodle on a board. Place chicken mixture on top and roll up to about the size of a large spring roll. Cut into 8 cm (3 in) lengths and place, seam downwards, on a saucer. Steam in a bamboo basket or other steamer for 15 minutes.

Serve garnished with shredded omelet and accompanied by soy sauce and chilli sauce.

Makes 15 rolls.

Note You may replace the chicken with prawns, oysters, duck, barbecued pork or other meats.

Velvet noodles

滑鷄麵 (WART GAI MEIN)

500 g (1 lb) fresh egg noodles, bought or home-made (see p. 83)
1 tablespoon sesame oil
2 tablespoons vegetable oil
1 clove garlic, crushed
2.5 cm (1 in) green ginger (see p. 100), crushed
10 dried mushrooms, soaked in warm water for 20 minutes
1 cup snow peas or green beans, blanched
1 cup sliced Chinese preserved green vegetable (see p. 103)
10 water chestnuts (see p. 105), sliced
½ cup sliced bamboo shoots (see p. 96)
½ cup stock
½ cooked chicken, sliced
2 tablespoons thin soy sauce
2 tablespoons oyster sauce (see p. 102)
coriander sprigs

Bring a large saucepan of water to the boil. (There should be enough water to cover the noodles.) Lower the noodles into the boiling water and cook for 10 minutes or until the noodles are tender. Remove and run cold water over them. Drain noodles and mix in the sesame oil.

Heat wok or frying pan and when hot add oil. Fry garlic and ginger until brown, then remove. Slice mushrooms and add them, plus snow peas, green vegetable, water chestnuts and bamboo shoots, to the wok or pan and cook for 3 minutes. Pour in the stock, add chicken, cover and simmer for 2 minutes.

Heat a clean wok or frying pan, add noodles and stir until heated. Mix in soy sauce and oyster sauce then place in a serving dish. Arrange chicken mixture on top and serve hot. Garnish with coriander sprigs.

Serves 4.

Seafood noodles

珍絲蟹麵 (JUN SEE HAI MEIN)

125 g (4 oz) cellophane noodles, soaked for 10 minutes

2 cups seasoned stock

¼ cup vegetable oil

2.5 cm (1 in) green ginger, shredded (see p. 100)

170 g (6 oz) raw seafood (your choice)

½ small tea melon, to make 2 cups cut into matchsticks (substitute choko, celery, bean sprouts or green beans)

1 teaspoon sugar

½ teaspoon salt

meat from 1 cooked crab, or 1 small can crab meat

1 tablespoon oyster sauce (see p. 102)

1 tablespoon thin soy sauce

2 eggs, made into an omelet and cut into fine strips

shallots for garnish

Cut cellophane noodles with scissors into 8 cm (3 in) lengths. Bring stock to the boil and cook noodles in it for 10 minutes. Drain, retaining stock.

Heat wok or frying pan and add oil. When hot fry ginger until browned then add raw seafood and stir until cooked. Remove to a platter.

Add more oil to wok if necessary, then fry tea melon (or substitute) lightly. Add sugar and salt. Pour in stock, return seafood to wok, add crab meat and heat through. Mix in cellophane noodles and add oyster sauce and soy sauce.

Serve hot with omelet on top. Garnish with strips of shallot.

Serves 4.

Note Canned abalone, sliced into matchsticks, can be substituted for the crab meat.

Long soup with hot sauce

湯麵 (TONG MEIN)

250 g (8 oz) fresh egg noodles, bought or home-made (see p. 83)
2 tablespoons vegetable oil
2.5 cm (1 in) green ginger, shredded (see p. 100)
1 clove garlic, crushed
250 g (8 oz) minced pork
2 teaspoons soy sauce
1 tablespoon brown bean paste (see p. 98)
½ teaspoon salt
1 teaspoon sesame oil
1 tablespoon hot bean sauce or chilli sauce, according to taste
1 cup beef stock
1 teaspoon extra sesame oil
2 teaspoons extra vegetable oil
1 egg, made into an omelet and shredded
chopped shallots

Bring a large saucepan of boiling water to the boil and cook noodles until soft. Rinse the noodles with warm water and drain.

Heat wok or frying pan, add oil, and when hot fry ginger and garlic until brown. Remove. Fry the pork until it changes colour, then mix in soy sauce, brown bean paste, salt, sesame oil and hot sauce. Pour in stock and cook for a further 2 minutes. Cover and allow to simmer for 5 minutes.

Mix sesame oil into the noodles. Heat wok or frying pan and when hot add vegetable oil. Heat noodles for 3 minutes.

Divide noodles into four servings and place each in the bottom of a deep serving bowl. Top with shredded egg and hot sauce and sprinkle with chopped shallots.

Serves 4.

Short soup

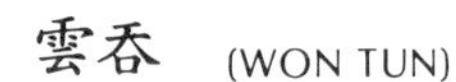

(WON TUN)

200 g (7 oz) lean and fat pork, finely minced
10 white ends of shallots
2 teaspoons soy sauce
½ teaspoon salt
1 teaspoon sesame oil
1 tablespoon peanut oil
30 *won tun* skins, 6 cm (2½ in) square (see p. 83)
1 beaten egg
1 tablespoon cornflour
seasoned soup
lettuce leaves
chopped shallots

Mince pork mince and shallots together finely until almost a paste. Stir in soy sauce, salt, sesame oil and peanut oil. Using a chopstick or ice cream stick, place about half a teaspoon of filling in the centre of each *won tun* skin. Seal the edges with beaten egg and fold over corner to corner.

Twist one corner to the top opposite corner and pull filling forward to form a 'cloud swallow' shape. Sprinkle with a little cornflour and cover until ready for use.

Makes 30 won tun.

If using for soup, bring soup to the boil in a large saucepan. Gently lower the *won tun* into the soup with a ladle. Cook for 5 minutes. Place lettuce leaves in the bottom of a soup bowl and ladle the hot soup into the bowl. Garnish with chopped shallots.

Or

Instead of being boiled, the *won tun* can be deep-fried and served with sweet and sour sauce.

King-size won tun

巨型雲吞 (SUI GOW)

250 g (8 oz) lean and fat pork, minced
10 water chestnuts (see p. 105)
10 white ends of shallots
1 tablespoon preserved vegetable (see p. 103)
1 teaspoon soy sauce
½ teaspoon salt
1 tablespoon sesame oil
¼ teaspoon white pepper
2.5 cm (1 in) green ginger, peeled and grated (see p. 100)
¼ cup pounded roasted sesame seeds
15 large *won tun* skins (see p. 83)
seasoned stock
1 beaten egg

Blend pork, water chestnuts, shallots and preserved vegetable together into a thick paste. Thoroughly mix in the soy sauce, salt, sesame oil, white pepper and ginger. Stir the sesame seeds into the mixture, then place in refrigerator to chill for 30 minutes.

Fill each pastry skin with 1 tablespoon of mixture and close the edges together, sealing with beaten egg as close to the filling as possible, so that there will be a 'frill' of pastry all around.

Boil a large quantity of water in a saucepan and carefully add the *sui gow* four or five at a time. They will rise to the top when cooked. Remove and place in individual soup bowls with lettuce or soft green vegetable on the bottom. Ladle hot seasoned stock over them. Accompany with a dip sauce (see p. 86).

Makes 15 sui gow.

Sweet Things

Cakes, Pastries & Biscuits

It is not generally known that the Chinese enjoy an enormous range of cakes, pastries and biscuits. Chinese sweets do not look or taste the same as those of the Western world. Nevertheless, they are immensely popular, and are made in such a way that if you cannot eat them immediately, they will keep for another day without any loss of quality. The biscuits can be kept fresh in airtight containers.

Like many people, the Chinese (who do not usually have large ovens in their kitchens) prefer to buy their cakes and pastries from the specialist. Still there is nothing more rewarding than 'doing your own thing' and if you can enjoy baking and are aware of some basic rules and kitchen techniques, your performance will be first class.

There are simple ways to make such things as the pastry for *darn* tarts (p. 68) — small tartlets which consist of crisp pastry with egg custard filling (quite sweet to the Chinese taste), baked until the pastry is golden brown and the custard has set. This process must have been thought up by some genius and has been used for generations in the production of *darn* tart, the most popular of all Chinese pastries. The dough is made in two separate parts. One part is placed on top of the other and the pastry is then rolled out and folded. Thus it differs from the French method of making puff pastry, which is made in one process and then rolled out and folded. The texture differs, too, in that the Chinese method results in a flaky yet soft pastry, compared with the flaky but brittle layers of French puff pastry. The Chinese method is simpler and more practical, because the strips of dough left over after cutting out the tarts can be laid on the next portion of dough to be rolled out and enveloped in the rolling and folding without detracting from the end result. This is often done by pastry chefs in the large restaurants that specialise in *darn* tarts as they make up such large quantities of dough that there are always strips left over. When these are gathered up and kneaded, the extra kneading tends to toughen the pastry. This same pastry is used for Curry puffs (p. 40) and Curried beef turnovers (p. 39), but the cutter traditionally used for these is larger than the one used for *darn* tarts.

Another ingenious method to avoid waste when making pastry is the method used for dim sims, *gow jees* and *shui mei*. After the pastry has been mixed and kneaded, the whole piece of dough is rolled with the palms of the hands into a long thin roll and then cut into uniform lengths. Each length of dough is rolled into a ball with the hands, then pressed with the flat side of a cleaver or rolled with a rolling pin into a thin round. This process eliminates any waste and also you can see at a glance the exact quantity at hand. If you were to roll out the dough and cut out the shapes with a round cutter, the left-over strips would probably be thrown away. Naturally, the dough could be gathered up and cut out again, but there would still usually be some waste.

This same process is used when making the yeast rounds for *char sieu bao* (Barbecued pork buns, p. 11). As the same recipe is used for enclosing sweet fillings too, put a dot of red vegetable colouring on top so that you can tell the difference. If you have made several kinds of buns, put two or four dots of red food colouring on top. This makes the buns even more attractive and helps you identify the different types.

Glutinous rice puffs

(for Chinese New Year and Lantern festivals)

煎堆 (JIN DOIH)

Basic dough

1 cup brown sugar
2 cups water
2 cups glutinous rice flour (see p. 100)
½ cup white sesame seeds
4 cups vegetable oil for deep-frying

Filling 1

(to make DOH SAR for New Year festival)
1 small can red bean purée

Filling 2

(to make LIN YOONG for Lantern festival)
1 small can lotus nut purée

Place the brown sugar and water in a small saucepan. Stir over moderate heat to dissolve the sugar. Allow to cool. Transfer to a large bowl.

Mix in the glutinous rice flour and knead slightly to form a ball of dough. Keep covered with a damp cloth until ready to use.

Divide the dough into 40 pieces and flatten each piece with the palm of the hand. Roll a teaspoon of the required filling into a ball and place one ball of filling in the centre of each dough round. Press edges together to close, then roll each dumpling into a ball. Sprinkle each with a little water, coat with sesame seeds and shake to remove excess seeds.

Heat vegetable oil in a wok or a deep saucepan until moderately hot and put two or three rice balls in at a time. Press each one firmly with a metal spoon or chopsticks (this enables the rice balls to swell evenly). As the rice balls continue to float to the surface, increase the heat and repeat the pressing process until the balls increase in size. Turn them continuously but do not press them after the outsides have become hard and golden brown. Remove and drain on absorbent paper.

Serve immediately, otherwise they will deflate and become chewy.

Makes 40 rice puffs.

Dragon Festival puddings

(for Dragon Boat festival)

 (JOONG)

4 cups glutinous rice

1 bundle dried lotus leaves (purchased in bundles)

string for tying lotus leaves

125 g (4 oz) streaky pork, salted and diced

125 g (4 oz) white or red soy beans, soaked in water overnight

1 tablespoon salt

10 salted duck egg yolks (see p. 44)

2 or 3 beaten eggs

4 tablespoons vegetable oil

Wash rice and soak for 1 hour or longer completely covered in water. Pour off water.

Soak lotus leaves and string in hot water for 20 minutes. Mix diced pork, soy beans and salt into the rice. Take three or four lotus leaves and form them into a cone shape. Spoon 4 tablespoons of rice mixture into the cone and press down with back of spoon. Press in a duck egg yolk and cover with rice mixture. Press down again. Close leaves over securely, using an extra leaf if necessary, and tie with string. Make sure that no rice is showing, or it will ooze out during cooking. Do the same with the rest of the lotus leaves, making about 10 cones in all.

Place puddings in a deep saucepan with enough water to cover and bring to the boil. Simmer for 3 or 4 hours. Leave overnight (standing in the water), then reheat for one hour next day.

To serve, remove lotus leaves, cut puddings into slices (using string) and accompany with small dishes of sugar; *or* cut into slices, dip in beaten egg and gently fry in vegetable oil until golden.

Makes 10 puddings, or 15 if made smaller (more duck eggs will of course be required).

Moon cakes (Cantonese-style)
(for Moon festival)

中秋月餅 (YIT GEONG BEANG)

This is an old family recipe. You will need to start preparations well in advance.

Pastry

4 cups flour
1 cup castor sugar
250 g (8 oz) lard
¾ cup peanut oil
1 beaten egg

Sift the flour into bowl and mix in the castor sugar. Work in the lard, then gradually stir in the peanut oil. Knead into a smooth dough. Cover with a clean cloth and allow to stand 20 minutes.

Turn dough out on to a board, knead lightly, then roll into a square sheet 2.5 cm (1 in) thick. Cut into 25 to 30 pieces. Knead each piece into a round ball then roll out until 8 cm (3 in) in diameter.

Filling

1 kg (2 lb) pork fat
3 tablespoons sugar
2 cups glutinous rice
3 cups castor sugar
¾ cup rose petal sugar (see p. 105)
2 or 3 cups water
2 cups slivered blanched almonds
2 cups white sesame seeds
2 cups olive nuts
1 cup crystallised mandarin peel
2 cups crystallised melon
12 salted duck egg yolks (p. 44)

Boil pork fat in enough water to cover for 15 minutes. Remove and allow to cool. Slice in thin sheets and preserve in layers with sugar for three weeks. Cut into small dice.

Roast glutinous rice on a tray in the oven, then grind into a fine powder. Place the ground rice in a large bowl. Mix in the castor sugar and sprinkle in the rose petal sugar. Add most of the water and stir to mix together. Mix in the almonds, sesame seeds, olive nuts and mandarin peel. If the mixture is too dry, add some more water. Mix in the diced pork fat and crystallised melon.

Turn the mixture out on to a tray and pack tightly together. Separate half the filling and mould into 12 rounded portions, making a hole in the centre of each one. Place a duck egg yolk in each hole and wrap pastry around securely. Make up the other half of filling with the balance of pastry (without duck egg yolks). Place in moon cake mould and shape by pressing and tilting from one side to the other to ensure that the moon cake filling has been evenly distributed. Turn out. Arrange on a greased baking tray, leaving space between the cakes to allow for spreading. Bake for 20 minutes in a hot oven, then take out and brush tops with beaten egg. Bake a further 10 minutes. Allow to cool.

Makes 25 to 30 moon cakes (half with duck egg, half without).

Coconut turnovers

椰子甜角 (YEAH GEE TIM GOCK)

25 *won tun* pastry skins, 6 cm (2½ in) square (p. 83)
1 beaten egg

Filling

1 cup finely shredded and chopped fresh coconut
½ cup chopped roasted peanuts
½ cup sugar
1 tablespoon toasted sesame seeds
4 cups vegetable oil for deep-frying

Mix all filling ingredients together. Place one teaspoon of filling in the centre of each *won tun* pastry skin. Fold over to form a triangle. Trim off corner to make a half moon shape. Brush the inner edge of turnover with beaten egg and press to seal securely.

Heat oil in a large wok or deep saucepan and deep-fry the turnovers until golden brown. Drain on absorbent paper.

Makes 25 turnovers.

Note Fresh coconut is desirable, but if not available use dehydrated shredded coconut, not desiccated coconut as it is too fine.

Peach buns

壽桃包 (SO TOW BAO)

1 packet bread dough mix or Basic steamed bread dough (p. 84)

Filling

1 small can red bean puree or 2 cups pitted, skinned and mashed dates
angelica (candied celery)
red food colouring
30 squares greaseproof paper

Make dough according to instructions on packet or recipe on page 84. Divide the dough into 30 pieces and flatten each piece with the palm of the hand.

Roll red bean puree or dates into 30 balls. Place one ball in the centre of each dough round. Press edges together to close, then roll into an oblong shape with a small point at one end. Using a chopstick or ice cream stick, make a small indentation in the side of each bun to resemble the crease in a peach.

Cut the angelica into long leaf shapes and stick two leaves to the bottom of each bun. Brush peaks of buns with red food colouring and place them on the squares of greaseproof paper, ready for steaming. Arrange in a steamer 2 cm (¾ in) apart and steam 15 to 20 minutes.

Makes 30 buns.

Steamed sponge cake

馬拉糕 (MAR LAI GOH)

4 large eggs
1 cup brown sugar
1 cup milk
½ teaspoon vanilla essence
2 tablespoons melted butter
2 cups flour
1 teaspoon baking powder

Beat eggs together with electric or manual beater and gradually blend in the sugar, until thick. Stir in milk, vanilla essence and melted butter. Fold in sifted flour and baking powder.

Pour into a greased square or oblong cake tin and steam in a bamboo basket or other steamer for 30 minutes. When cool, cut into large slices.

Cantonese-style sponge cake

鷄蛋糕 (GAI DARN BEANG)

5 eggs
1 cup castor sugar
1¼ cups self-raising flour
1 tablespoon water
¼ cup desiccated coconut

Beat eggs together with an electric or manual beater, and gradually add the sugar until the mixture is thick and just at the stage when it will slowly drip from the beater.

Fold in flour and water. Gently mix in the desiccated coconut.

Grease a square or oblong cake tin and line it with greased wax paper. Pour in the batter and steam in a bamboo basket or other steamer for 30 minutes. Allow to cool and cut into sections.

Hot strawberry ice cream logs

果子雪糕 (YIT HOONG GWOR SIT GO)

1 litre carton strawberry ice cream
2 eggs, plus 2 extra yolks
½ cup thin cream
breadcrumbs (*panko*, see p. 98)
cornflour for dusting
vegetable oil for deep-frying
½ cup whipped cream
8 fresh strawberries

Cut ice cream into short logs about 2.5 cm (1 in) in diameter. Roll slightly on a board to make the logs round. Place immediately in the freezer to keep firm.

Beat eggs and egg yolks with thin cream in a large shallow bowl. Spread breadcrumbs on a plate. Take the ice cream logs from the freezer and dust with cornflour, using a small sieve or tea strainer. Dip the floured logs in the beaten egg mixture and roll in breadcrumbs. Return to tray and freeze again.

Just before serving, heat oil in wok or saucepan. Moisten a ladle with the hot fat. Place a log in the ladle and deep-fry until golden brown all over. Drain on absorbent paper. Serve on a plate with a spoonful of whipped cream and a strawberry on top.

Makes about 8 ice cream logs.

Note Logs can be breadcrumbed in advance and kept in freezer until ready to serve.

Water chestnut slices

馬蹄糕 (MAR TAI GOH)

500 g (1 lb) fresh water chestnuts or 1 small can water chestnuts (see p. 105)
2 cups castor sugar
10 cups water
2 cups water chestnut powder (see p. 105)
¼ cup corn oil
2 tablespoons vegetable oil

Peel, wash and slice the water chestnuts. (If canned, drain and slice.) Mix water chestnuts with sugar and 5 cups of the water and bring to the boil. Stir the water chestnut powder with the other 5 cups of water. Blend into the heated mixture and allow to simmer. Add corn oil and bring to the boil. Turn off heat and pour into a well-greased swiss roll tin. Steam for 1 hour. When cool, cut into small squares or slices.

Heat wok or frying pan, and when hot add vegetable oil and lightly fry the slices until golden. Serve hot or cold.

Makes about 20 slices.

Agar-agar and jelly dessert

杏仁豆腐 (DAI CHOY GOR)

30 g (1 oz) agar-agar (see p. 96)
5 cups water
¼ cup sugar
1 cup milk
½ teaspoon vanilla essence
100 g (3½ oz) packet jelly crystals
1 cup fruit syrup from canned mixed fruit
fruits in season

Separate strands of agar-agar and wash thoroughly in cool water. Squeeze dry and place in a saucepan with the water. Heat through until dissolved, stirring continuously. Strain through a cheesecloth and return to saucepan. Lower heat and stir in the sugar and milk. Mix in the vanilla essence. Cook another 3 or 4 minutes. Do not allow to boil. Pour into a flat tray and allow to set. Cut into small cubes or other shapes and place in a large serving bowl.

Make up jelly crystals using less water than usual, so as to make a firm jelly. Cut up and mix with agar-agar and fruit syrup.

Serve chilled with canned fruit or any fruits in season.

Serves 8.

Lemon grass jelly and ice cream

涼粉雪糕 (LOONG FUN SIT GO)

1 can lemon grass jelly (see p. 102)
1 litre carton lime ice cream

Remove both ends of lemon jelly can and slip the jelly out in one piece. Cut into small dice and place in a glass dish. Chill.

When ready to serve, scoop out lime ice cream and place on top of lemon jelly.

Serves 8.

Egg custard (*darn*) tarts

蛋撻

Number 1 pastry
1 cup flour
250 g (8 oz) lard

Number 2 pastry
¾ cup flour
1 egg
½ cup cold water
30 g (1 oz) firm butter

Custard filling
6 eggs
2½ cups milk
2 cups sugar
½ teaspoon vanilla essence
½ teaspoon egg yellow food colouring

Sift flour for number 1 pastry on to a board. Work in lard and knead into a soft dough. Place in refrigerator to chill.

Sift flour for number 2 pastry on to a board. Make a well in the centre and mix in the egg and water. Work in butter and knead gently. Place in refrigerator to chill.

To make up the pastry, wrap number 2 pastry around number 1 pastry and roll out to 2.5 cm (1 in) thick. Fold both ends to meet at centre. Roll out and repeat the process three more times. Roll out until 5 mm (¼ in) thick. Use a fluted pastry cutter to match the size of the moulds you will use for baking. Grease the moulds and line with pastry, pressing it down lightly.

Beat eggs together lightly then stir in milk and sugar. Add vanilla essence and colouring. Strain to obtain a very smooth mixture.

Spoon the strained egg custard into pastry shells and bake them in a hot oven for 20 to 30 minutes, or until the custard is firm and the pastry is golden brown. Remove from moulds and allow to cool slightly. Serve warm.

Makes 18 darn *tarts.*

Noodle twists

蛋散 (DARN SARN)

500 g (1 lb) sheet flour noodle or large *won tun* pastry skins (p. 83)
3 cups vegetable oil
icing sugar

Cut the noodle into strips 10 × 4 cm (4 × 1½ in), or cut the *won tun* skins in half. With a sharp knife, make three slits along the centre of each piece of noodle 4 cm (1½ in) long. Holding one end firmly, pull the other end of the noodle through the centre slit, thus making the 'twist'. Keep covered with a damp cloth until ready for deep-frying.

Heat oil in wok or large saucepan. Deep-fry twists a few at a time until golden brown. Sprinkle with icing sugar. Store in an airtight container when cold.

Makes about 80 twists.

Crisp almond biscuits

杏仁酥餅 (HUNG YUN SOO BEANG)

3½ cups flour
1 teaspoon baking soda
1½ cups castor sugar
170 g (6 oz) lard
3 eggs
1 teaspoon almond essence
½ cup blanched almonds
1 egg
1 tablespoon milk

Sift flour and baking soda into a bowl and mix in sugar. Make a well in the centre and dot the flour with lumps of lard. Break eggs into the centre and add almond essence. Work with hands to form a dough.

On a board, roll the dough into a long roll 4.5 cm (1½ in) in diameter. Cut evenly into 35 pieces. Roll each piece into a small ball and make a small indentation on top. Press a blanched almond in centre. Arrange biscuits on a lightly greased baking tray, spacing them out to allow for spreading. Beat the egg with the milk and brush tops with the mixture. Bake in a moderate oven for 20 minutes until golden brown.

Remove and allow to cool. Keep stored in an airtight container.

Makes 35 biscuits.

Sesame cookies

芝麻餅 (JEE MAR BEANG)

3 cups plain flour
1 teaspoon baking powder
350 g (12 oz) shortening (lard, margarine and/or butter)
1¼ cups castor sugar
½ teaspoon almond essence
1 beaten egg
½ teaspoon lime water (see p. 102)
1 beaten egg
¼ cup sesame seeds

Sift flour and baking soda together. Cream shortening and castor sugar together until fluffy, then mix in the almond essence and beaten egg thoroughly. Add lime water. Stir in the flour and baking soda.

Turn dough out on to a board and form into a long thin roll. Cut into 2.5 cm (1 in) lengths. Place the pieces of dough on a lightly greased baking tray, spaced out to allow for spreading. Press the tops flat with a fork and brush with beaten egg. Sprinkle with sesame seeds and bake in a moderate oven for about 15 minutes.

Allow to cool, then store in an airtight container.

Makes about 36 biscuits.

Home-made Wines & Teas

Making Wines

It is comparatively easy to make wines at home. There are no special skills required for this fascinating hobby, only a great deal of patience. However, there are a few points that must be taken into account to ensure success.

- The water should be boiled before it is added to any recipe.
- Any yeast is suitable, whether dried, tinned or fresh. The yeast should be creamed together with a little sugar and dissolved in warm water before it is added to the brew. Never add the yeast until the brew has cooled to blood heat.
- Do not use any kind of metal receptacle for fermenting wines; use instead a large china or earthenware container, or even a plastic bucket. Always keep the container covered with a damp cloth during the fermentation period.
- Sterilise the bottles for holding the wine and cool them before filling with wine. Fill to 4 cm (1½ in) from the top of the neck of the bottle and cork lightly. Only new corks should be used. (Do not use metal clip-on sealers.)
- After bottling, the wine will continue to clear and will form a crust in the bottle. You may decant carefully into dry, clean bottles as often as you wish.
- Wine ages best at a constant low temperature. When you are quite sure the wine is quiescent, lay the bottles with the necks resting on a bar of wood, so that the wine just touches the cork.

Garm boui! (Bottoms up!)

Chinese Teas

Tea drinking is considered an art by the Chinese, and it takes many years to become a connoisseur. The tea is infused in boiling water, and petals or leaves from the plum, rose, lychee, jasmine or chrysanthemum may be added to make a fragrant brew. Medicinal teas may be made by infusing herbs and seeds. Chinese tea is consumed from tiny cups without handles. Some have lids to keep the tea warm in the winter months.

The Chinese believe that drinking a lot of tea helps to keep the complexion clear and fine, and also cleanses the system, particularly after a large meal, when a hot cup of tea has a soothing effect on the system.

All tea comes from the same plant, and it is only the different processes that the tender tea leaves undergo that dictate the classification into types. The finest tea grows high in the mountains, where the morning dew can settle on the young leaves. Monkeys are trained to pick the leaves.

Teas are consumed for different purposes. If one feels a cold coming on, it is time for a medicinal tea, such as *gum mor cha*, and bitter teas. The highly scented teas are for poets and romantics. The more mildly scented teas are served after banquets, and ordinary black, red and green teas are sipped throughout the day.

There are also sweet teas made with pounded nuts and seed pods such as almonds (see recipe on page 77), lotus seeds and walnuts, which are served warm in a bowl and eaten with a spoon. They are usually served towards the end of a banquet.

Rice wine

米酒 (MEI JO)

1.5 kg (3 lb) short grain or glutinous rice
1.5 kg (3 lb) sugar
500 g (1 lb) raisins, finely chopped
4.5 litres (8 pints) water
30 g (1 oz) fresh yeast
extra sugar
warm water

Put rice, sugar and raisins in the fermenting container. Boil the water and allow it to cool until lukewarm. Pour it into the rice mixture container. Cream the yeast with a little sugar and warm water and stir it into the rice mixture.

Allow to stand for 8 to 9 days, stirring on the first 3 days. Strain and bottle. Lay down for 5 or 6 months before drinking.

Makes 6 bottles.

Ginger wine

羗酒 (GEUNG JO)

250 g (8 oz) fresh ginger, scraped (see p. 100)
60 g (2 oz) raisins, finely chopped
750 g (1½ lb) sugar
7 litres (12 pints) water
grated rind and juice of 2 large lemons
30 g (1 oz) fresh yeast

Gently crush the ginger with a mallet or the flat side of a cleaver. Place ginger, raisins and sugar in a large pot with the water and bring to the boil, then simmer for 1 hour. Skim off any scum as it forms.

Remove from heat and stir in the grated lemon rind. Pour into fermenting container and allow to cool until lukewarm. Cream the yeast, using a little of the liquid to moisten it, and add it to the ginger mixture. Stir well and leave for 24 hours.

Add the lemon juice and stir daily until fermentation ceases, which should be after about 2 weeks. Strain and bottle. Lay down for 3 to 4 months before drinking.

Makes 6 to 8 bottles.

Barley wine

薏米酒 (EE-MEI JO)

500 g (1 lb) barley
500 g (1 lb) raisins, finely chopped
500 g (1 lb) potatoes, washed, scrubbed and sliced
2 kg (4 lb) sugar
4.5 litres (8 pints) water
30 g (1 oz) fresh yeast
extra sugar
warm water

Place barley, raisins, potatoes and sugar in the fermenting container. Boil the water and allow it to cool until lukewarm. Pour it into the container. Cream the yeast with a little sugar and warm water and stir it into the barley mixture.

Allow to stand for 3 weeks, stirring daily. Strain and bottle. Leave the corks loose for a week, then close tightly.

Lay down for at least 6 months before drinking.

Makes 6 bottles.

Banana wine

蕉酒 (JEW JO)

1 ½ kg (3 lb) bananas
2.8 litres (5 pints) water
1½ kg (3 lb) sugar
50 g (2 oz) fresh yeast
120 g (4 oz) raisins, finely chopped
extra sugar
warm water

Peel and slice the bananas and put them into the fermenting container. Boil water and allow to cool until lukewarm. Pour 2 litres (8 cups) of water over the bananas. Stir in 500 g (1 lb) sugar. Cream the yeast with a little sugar and warm water and add to the banana mixture. Leave covered for 1 week, then strain, pressing all the liquid from the bananas.

Make a syrup with the rest of the sugar and water and pour it into the container. Add chopped raisins and allow to ferment for 7 to 10 days. When fermentation ceases, strain and bottle. Lay down for 9 months before drinking.

Makes 5 or 6 bottles.

Coconut wine

椰子酒 (YEAH JEE JO)

4.5 litres (8 pints) fresh coconut milk (see p. 88)
1.5 kg (3 lb) sugar
rind of 1 lemon, finely peeled
rind of 1 orange, finely peeled
250 g (8 oz) raisins, finely chopped
30 g (1 oz) fresh yeast
extra sugar
warm water

Boil the coconut milk with the sugar and lemon and orange rinds. Skim off any scum from the surface and pour into fermenting container. Mix in the raisins.

Allow mixture to cool until lukewarm. Cream yeast with a little sugar and warm water and add to the coconut milk mixture. Allow to stand for 1 week, then strain and bottle. Cork lightly and leave for 2 weeks.

Decant carefully, re-bottle and cork lightly and leave for 2 more weeks. Then cork firmly and lay down for 6 to 12 months or more before drinking.

Makes 6 bottles.

Almond tea

杏仁茶 (HUNG YUN CHA)

¼ cup almond powder
½ cup sugar
6 cups water
½ teaspoon almond essence
2 tablespoons cornflour, blended with a little water
½-1 cup thin cream
2 tablespoons toasted almond slivers

Bring the almond powder, sugar and water to the boil in a large saucepan. Keep stirring until the sugar dissolves. Stir in the almond essence and the blended cornflour. Simmer until the mixture is smooth. Remove from heat. Mix in the thin cream thoroughly.

Pour into individual bowls and top with fine slivers of toasted almonds.

Serves 6.

Reference Recipes

Dim sim pastry

點心皮 (DEEM SUM PEI)

3 cups plain flour
1 cup (approximately) hot water
1 tablespoon vegetable oil
¼ teaspoon salt (optional)
cornflour for dusting

Sift flour on to a board and make a well in it. Pour in the hot water and oil and add salt. Form into a dough, then knead lightly until smooth and glossy. Put the dough in a greased bowl, cover with a clean cloth and allow to stand for 20 minutes.

Dust board with cornflour and knead dough into a long thin roll. Cut off even pieces, shape into balls, and roll each ball out to make thin pastry rounds 6 cm (2½ in) in diameter. Sprinkle each round with cornflour and stack them on top of each other. Keep covered with plastic food wrap until ready for use.

Makes about 30 rounds.

Shui mei pastry

燒賣皮 (SHUI MEI PEI)

2 cups strong bread flour or semolina flour (or 1¾ cups plain flour and ¼ cup gluten)
1 cup boiling water
cornflour for dusting

Sift the flour into a deep bowl and make a well in the centre. Slowly pour in the boiling water and work into a dough using a wooden spoon or chopsticks.

When the dough is cool, knead well and then transfer to a board which has been dusted with cornflour. Continue to knead until the dough is elastic. Roll the dough into a long shape with your hands until it is approximately 2.5 cm (1 in) in diameter, then cut it into about 30 pieces and press them into rounds. Roll the rounds until they are about 6 cm (2½ in) in diameter. They are now ready to hold the filling for *shui mei*.

Keep the rounds covered with plastic food wrap until ready for use, or they will dry up and become brittle and will not hold the filling successfully.

Makes about 30 rounds..

Gow jee pastry

餃子皮 (GOW JEE PEI)

2 cups plain flour
½ teaspoon salt
¾ cup (approximately) hot water
2 tablespoons cornflour

Sift flour into a deep bowl. Add salt. Gradually pour in the hot water, stirring continuously with chopsticks or a wooden spoon to form a dough. Sprinkle cornflour on to board and knead dough for 5 minutes. Cover with a moist teatowel or plastic food wrap and allow to stand for 20 minutes.

Knead again until the dough is elastic in texture, then form it into a long roll. Cut into about 24 pieces and roll each piece into a round 8 cm (3 in) in diameter. Keep covered with plastic food wrap until ready for use.

Makes about 24 rounds.

Har gow pastry

蝦餃皮 (HAR GOW PEI)

1 454 g (1 lb) packet Chinese wheat starch (see p. 106)
½ teaspoon salt
3 cups (approximately) boiling water
1 tablespoon peanut oil

Empty the wheat starch into a deep bowl. Add salt. Pour the boiling water in the centre and stir vigorously with chopsticks or a wooden spoon to make a dough. Turn dough out on working board and when cool enough to handle knead in the peanut oil until the dough is smooth and elastic. The dough must not be dry. Divide it into two sections and roll into a long strip 2.5 cm (1 in) in diameter. Keep covered with a moist tea towel or plastic food wrap until ready for use.

Cut off small sections from the long strip and shape into balls. Roll each ball into a round 2.5 cm (1 in) across or flatten into shape with the side of a cleaver, lightly oiled. You may find it easier to place the dough ball between two sheets of oiled greaseproof paper before flattening with the cleaver or a rolling pin.

Shape and fill as described on pages 6 and 7. If liked, some or all of the rounds can be wrapped in plastic and frozen for later use.

Makes about 24 rounds.

Fun gor pastry

粉果皮 (FUN GOR PEI)

1 454 g (1 lb) packet Chinese wheat starch (see p. 106)
½ teaspoon salt
2 cups (approximately) boiling water
1 teaspoon vegetable oil

Mix the wheat starch and salt in a deep bowl. Pour in boiling water as needed and mix continuously with a wooden spoon or chopsticks until the mixture becomes a soft, dry dough. It should not be too wet. Knead lightly in bowl for 5 minutes. Brush a little oil across the top, cover with a moist teatowel or plastic food wrap and allow to stand for 20 minutes.

A marble surface is ideal for rolling out the dough, but if one is not available, lightly grease a pastry board and roll dough into a long thin roll about 2.5 cm (1 in) in diameter. Cut into 2.5 cm (1 in) rounds and roll each into an 8 cm (3 in) circle, or press into shape with the flat side of a cleaver, lightly oiled. Fill with *fun gor* (p. 8) or other filling.

Makes about 24 rounds.

Spring roll pastry (large)

春卷皮 (CHOON GUERN PEI)

3 cups plain flour
½ teaspoon salt
1½ cups cold water

Sift flour and salt together in a bowl. Gradually add water, mixing thoroughly. Mix until smooth. Spoon 2 tablespoons water over the batter and allow to stand for 1 to 1½ hours. Bubbles should form around the edge.

Lift batter from around edge and mix into batter in the centre of bowl. Repeat this process 3 or 4 times until batter is smooth and elastic. Sprinkle water on batter to keep it moist.

Heat an omelette pan or small frying pan until medium hot. Wipe over with an oil soaked cloth. Take a ladle of batter and thinly coat bottom of pan. Lower heat and cook slowly until edges begin to curl. Do not allow to brown.

Peel off pastry skin from pan and place over an inverted saucer to cool. Repeat this process until all batter is used.

Makes about 10 rounds.

Won tun pastry (large)

雲呑皮 (WON TUN PEI)

2 cups plain flour
$\frac{2}{3}$ cup boiling water
1 teaspoon vegetable oil

Sift flour into a bowl. Pour in half the water, then the oil, then the rest of the water. Mix quickly with chopsticks or a wooden spoon to form a dough. Turn the dough out on to a floured board and knead lightly until smooth and glossy. Return to lightly greased bowl and allow to stand for 20 minutes.

Dust the board with flour and form dough into a long roll 2.5 cm (1 in) in diameter. Cut into 2.5 cm (1 in) pieces and roll each piece into a ball. Flatten with the hands, then roll out into squares 10 × 10 cm (4 × 4 in). Sprinkle each one lightly with flour and wrap in greaseproof paper until ready for use.

Makes about 15 squares.

Note For smaller *won tun* skins, form dough into a long roll 2 cm (¾ in) in diameter and cut into 2 cm pieces, to make 6 cm (2½ in) squares.

Home-made egg noodles

 (EE MEIN)

4 cups strong bread flour (or 3 cups plain flour and 1 cup gluten)
12 eggs
1 tablespoon water
1 teaspoon salt
8-10 tablespoons vegetable oil

Sift flour on to a board. Make a well in the centre, break in the eggs and add water and salt. Gradually work the eggs into the flour to make a smooth dough. Knead and roll out with a pastry machine until very thin. Divide the noodles into 8 or 10 bundles and form each into a ring. Heat oil in wok or frying pan and when hot lightly fry each bundle of noodles on both sides. Drain on absorbent paper.

When cold, store in an airtight container.

Makes 8 or 10 bundles.

Note It is advisable to use good quality vegetable oil as an inferior oil, e.g. coconut, will turn the noodles rancid if they have to be stored.

Basic steamed bread dough

麵包 (MIN BAO)

8 cups plain flour
2 tablespoons lard or margarine
2 tablespoons sugar
1 7 g (¼ oz) packet dried yeast
1 teaspoon vegetable oil

Sift flour on to a board and work in lard or margarine. Dissolve sugar in the warm water and mix in the yeast. Allow to stand for 10 minutes. Make a well in the flour and work in the yeast mixture. Knead into a smooth dough. Lightly grease a large bowl with vegetable oil and place the dough in it. Cover the bowl with a tea-towel and keep in a warm place until it has doubled in bulk (approximately 40 minutes). Knead dough once more, and allow to rise again.

Turn dough on to a board, and divide into two sections. Roll out until 1 cm (⅜ in) thick and cut into rounds 5 cm (2 in) in diameter. Alternatively the dough can be frozen for use at a later date.

Makes about 40 rounds.

Home-made rice noodles

(a substitute for rice noodle pastry)

(FUN)

2 cups plain flour
1 tablespoon cornflour
1 teaspoon salt
2 tablespoons vegetable oil
1¼ cups cool water

Mix flour, cornflour and salt together. While stirring, gradually add vegetable oil and water. (Alternatively, if preferred, combine all ingredients with an electric mixer.) Strain mixture to produce a smooth batter.

Lightly grease a sponge cake tin and pour in a small amount of batter to cover the surface thinly. Steam, covered, for 2 or 3 minutes. Remove and allow to cool. Loosen the edges with a knife and roll the *fun* into a thin roll.

Grease the sponge cake tin again (or use several tins) and steam until all the mixture is used.

Makes 12 to 15 rolls.

Note When rolls are served cold, cut up into small lengths and serve with Soy sauce dip (p. 87) and vegetable oil mixed together. Toasted sesame seeds may be added to the dip. *Fun* can be used in any noodle recipe.

Roast duck

燒鴨 (SIEU AP)

1 fat duck
5 cups hot water
3 tablespoons soy sauce
1 tablespoon honey
1 teaspoon sugar
¼ cup vegetable oil
2 tablespoons sherry
few drops red food colouring
½ cup chicken stock *or* water

Clean duck well and pour hot water over a few times to plump. Allow to dry.

Mix soy sauce, honey, sugar, vegetable oil, sherry and red colouring in a large bowl.

Add duck to soy sauce mixture and marinate for 30 minutes, turning occasionally to ensure even colouring.

Remove duck from bowl and place on aluminium foil over a roasting rack. Place rack in baking dish containing stock or water.

Roast in a moderate oven for approximately 15 minutes per 500 g (1 lb) of duck. After the first 20 minutes, when duck is browned, cover with aluminium foil and cook for a further 20 minutes. Remove foil to complete cooking.

Barbecued pork

叉燒 (CHAR SIEU)

1 kg (2 lb) pork loin
1 teaspoon salt
1 tablespoon hoisin sauce (see p. 101)
2 teaspoons sugar
2 tablespoons soy sauce
1 tablespoon tomato sauce
2 cloves garlic, crushed
¼ cup rosé or sherry
2 tablespoons honey melted in ½ cup hot water

Cut pork into thick strips 5 cm (2 in) wide and any length (to suit size of oven). Rub in salt. Marinate in hoisin sauce, sugar, soy sauce, tomato sauce, garlic and rosé or sherry for 1 hour or longer.

Brush on melted honey, then barbecue, roast or hang pork strips with hooks from the top shelf in the oven, with a pan below to catch the drippings. Cook for 30-40 minutes at a moderate temperature. (If desired, thread the pork strips on a rôtisserie and cook at a moderate temperature for 30-40 minutes.)

Dip sauce for sui gow

水餃汁 (SUI GOW JUP)

2 tablespoons soy sauce
1 teaspoon sartee sauce
½ teaspoon sesame oil
2 teaspoons hot peanut oil

Mix soy sauce and sartee sauce together, then add sesame oil. Dribble hot peanut oil on top.

Hoisin dip sauce

海鮮汁 (HOISIN JUP)

2 tablespoons hoisin sauce
1 tablespoon pounded roasted sesame seeds
1 teaspoon finely chopped white ends of shallot
1 tablespoon hot peanut oil

Mix hoisin sauce with pounded sesame seeds and finely chopped shallots. Dribble hot peanut oil on top.

Sartee sauce

沙爹汁 (SARTEE JUP)

6 small red hot chillies
2 cloves garlic
1 small onion
4 candlenuts
½ cup peanut oil
100 g (3½ oz) ground raw peanuts
¼ cup lemon juice
1 cup water
4 tablespoons sugar
1 teaspoon salt

Pound or grind together chillies, garlic, onion and candlenuts.

Heat peanut oil in a wok or pan and fry ground ingredients for 5 minutes. Stir in ground peanuts and lemon juice. Add water, sugar and salt. Allow to simmer for 5 minutes or until sauce thickens.

Soy sauce dip

醬油汁 (JEUNG YAU JUP)

1 tablespoon soy sauce
1 teaspoon hot vegetable oil
½ teaspoon sesame oil
½ teaspoon toasted sesame seeds (optional)

Mix soy sauce and oils together. Place in small bowl and sprinkle with toasted sesame seeds, if liked.

Sweet and sour sauce

甜酸醬 (TIM SIN JEUNG)

1 onion, chopped
1 capsicum, diced
1 cup pineapple pieces
2 tablespoons cornflour blended with ½ cup water or stock
1 tablespoon wine vinegar
2 tablespoons sugar
1 teaspoon soy sauce
1 teaspoon tomato sauce
⅓ cup pineapple juice
¼ teaspoon salt
½ teaspoon sesame oil

Fry onion in a small saucepan until transparent (do not brown). Add capsicum and pineapple. Pour in the remaining ingredients and stir over slow heat until thickened.

Coconut milk from fresh coconut

There is an implement designed for this purpose. It is shaped in a half-curve, one end to be clamped on a solid surface and at the curved end is a sharp cutter with grooves on the ends. The coconut is peeled of its fibres, and broken in half. (The water in the coconut is not the coconut milk.) The half of the coconut is pushed against the sharp end, and the flesh is churned out. This grated flesh is then covered with about 2 cups of warm water, mixed together well by hand, and allowed to stand. All the white liquor is then squeezed out into a bowl; this becomes the fresh coconut cream; when warm water is added to the flesh of the coconut for a second time, it is coconut milk.

Coconut milk from desiccated coconut

¼ pound desiccated coconut
warm water

Place desiccated coconut in a large bowl and pour in 1 cup warm water. Allow to stand 30 minutes. Using a fine sieve, squeeze all the liquor from the coconut or use a fine piece of muslin over the sieve to prevent any particle of coconut seeping through. This first liquor is called the coconut cream. Using the residue of desiccated coconut, pour in another cup or even 2 cups of warm water and allow to stand 30 minutes. Squeeze out the liquor again, and this becomes the coconut milk.

Suggested Menus

Menu 1

1 basket Dim sims (4 pieces) (pp.5, 6, 23, 24)
1 basket Prawn dumplings (4 pieces) (pp.6, 7)
1 basket *Gow jees* (4 pieces) (p.25)
2 baskets Red yam puffs (2 pieces per basket) (p.32)
2 servings Braised spare ribs (p.42)
2 servings Savoury buns (4 pieces) (pp.11, 12, 13)
2 servings Chicken wings in soy sauce (p.37)
Chicken chow mein (p.49)
Darn tarts (p.68)
Tea (pp.74, 77)

Menu 2

1 basket Dim sims (4 pieces) (pp.5, 23, 24)
1 basket *Shui mei* (4 pieces) (p.9)
1 basket Prawn dumplings (4 pieces) (pp.6, 7)
1 basket Miniature dim sims (4 pieces) (p.6)
2 servings fried *won tun* with sweet and sour sauce (p.54)
2 servings Chicken and mushroom buns (4 pieces) (p.13)
2 servings Diced bread prawn balls (4 pieces) (p.33)
2 servings Oyster sauce roast pork (p.42)
Braised noodles (p.48)
Lemon grass jelly and ice cream (p.67)
Tea (pp.74, 77)

Menu 3

1 basket Dim sims (4 pieces) (pp.5, 6, 23, 24)
1 basket *Shui mei* (4 pieces) (p.9)
1 basket Prawn dumplings (4 pieces) (pp.6, 7)
2 servings Prawn sticks (p.34)
2 servings Meat balls with sheet bean curd (p.7)
2 servings Savoury buns (4 pieces) (pp.11, 12, 13)
2 basins Glutinous rice and chicken (p.14)
2 servings Braised spare ribs (p.42)
2 servings Curry puffs (4 pieces) (p.40)
2 servings Water chestnut slices (4 pieces) (p. 66)
Braised noodles (p.48)
Agar-agar and jelly dessert (p.67)
Tea (pp.74, 77)

Menu 4

1 basket Dim sims (4 pieces) (pp.5, 6, 23, 24)
1 basket *Shui mei* (4 pieces) (p.9)
1 basket Prawn dumplings (4 pieces) (pp.6, 7)
2 servings Diced bread prawn balls (4 pieces) (p. 33)
2 servings Savoury buns (4 pieces) (p.11, 12, 13)
2 servings Chicken and ham rolls (4 pieces) (p.30)
2 servings Gourmet spring rolls (4 pieces) (p.26)
2 servings Chicken wings in soy sauce (p.37)
Rice noodles (pp.50, 84)
Hot strawberry ice-cream logs (p.66)
Tea (pp.74, 77)

Glossary

OF CHINESE INGREDIENTS

Agar-agar

大菜糕 (DAI CHO GOR)

Derived from seaweed. When the seaweed is burned, the ashes are called 'kelp' which is the chief source of iodine. From the organic portion of the seaweed which remains is a substance called alginic acid, one of the most versatile of natural products. Alginic acid produces an edible gelatine-like substance, a solution of which is used for thickening purposes. It will set at room temperature. This is spun into long threads and allowed to dry out. Sold in bundles as agar-agar, it is used to set jelly-like confectionery and for thickening soups and sauces.

Bamboo shoots

竹筍 (DOOK SOON)

Only the young shoots are used for food, and they are boiled until tender. The canned variety is already cooked and can be used straight from the can, sliced or diced, according to the recipe.

Bean curd

豆腐 (TAOFU)

This is a bland, smooth, custardy substance, rich in protein, made by cooking, mashing and pressing white soy beans. It can be bought fresh or canned. Bean curd is steamed, fried, deep-fried, braised and used for soups.

Bean curd, thin sheets

腐皮 (FOI BIN FOO JOOK)

Brittle, paper-thin sheets of bean curd which are of first quality. Used as an outer covering to enclose other food. Soak in warm water for 15 to 20 minutes before using.

Black beans (crushed)

豆豉 (DOW SEE)

These are black soy beans that have been salted and spiced. They come in packets or cans and are extremely salty. When purchased in their dry state they must be washed before use. The canned variety need not be washed. If the recipe calls for chopped or mashed black beans, these are more economical than whole black beans (*ooh dow*).

Black beans (whole)

烏豆 (OOH DOW)

These are also known by the name of *dow see*, which are black soy beans that have been salted and spiced. When purchased as *ooh dow* they are whole and not broken up. They have a very strong aroma which disappears when cooking and leaves a mild appetising flavour.

Breadcrumbs
麵衣 (PANKO)

Panko are Japanese breadcrumbs. They differ from ordinary breadcrumbs in that they are in larger pieces and tend to make the finished product larger and knobbly in appearance.

Brown bean paste
麵豉醬 (MIN SEE JEUNG)

This is a sweet bean paste that can be purchased in small cans or jars. It is made with partly crushed soy beans and flavoured with spices and other seasonings. It imparts a very distinctive flavour to whatever it accompanies and there is no substitute that would be satisfactory. *Min see jeung* will keep indefinitely in the refrigerator.

Caul fat
豬網 (JEE MONG)

A transparent net-like fatty tissue used as a covering for chicken rolls or to wrap ingredients ready to be deep-fried. Part of the great omentum of the pig (see also pork caul).

Celery cabbage
黄芽白 (WONG AH BARK)

This is a delicate green, closely packed cabbage with white stems which resembles a large bunch of celery. It has endless uses and may be cooked or eaten raw. When shredded finely it is excellent for spring rolls. In Japanese cooking this cabbage is used extensively, especially for *sukiyaki*.

Cellophane noodles

粉絲 (FUN SEE)

These are fine, transparent bean starch noodles. The different processes of cooking the noodles result in a particular texture and taste. When soaked in water they become limp, and when plunged in hot oil they immediately puff up and form a white, crisp mass of noodles.

Chinese parsley

芫荽 (YIN SAY)

Also known as cilantro or fresh coriander. This herb is a very tasty addition to any dish. The stalks can be used in soups and the delicate green leaves used as a garnish.

Chinese sausage

臘腸 (LARP CHONG)

These sausages are approximately 15 cm (6 in) long and are made in pairs and strung together. The different types are pork, chicken liver, duck liver, or a combination of these meats. (Fish sausages are now gradually appearing on the market, too.) The only preparation required is to wipe them with a warm cloth and steam for 10 minutes. If they are to be used in a rice dish they are placed on top of the rice for the last 5 minutes of steaming.

Dried shrimps
蝦米 (HAR MEI)

An expensive item today, owing to the high price of seafood, although when the shrimps are dehydrated they shrink and are very light in weight relative to their volume. They must be soaked in warm water for up to 1 hour before use. The flavour is very distinctive when used in conjunction with eggs and vegetables.

Five-spice powder
五香粉 (HEUNG LO FUN)

This well-known blend of five spices is considered by the Chinese to be a masterpiece of blending. It consists of a mixture of Chinese aniseed, cloves, cinnamon, anise herb and the aromatic seeds of fennel. Five-spice powder gives a wonderful aroma to food, particularly chicken and pork dishes. It must be used with discretion as it is not intended to overwhelm the flavours in the dish, but has the ability of making a simple dish into one in the gourmet class.

Fresh (green) ginger
薑 (GEUNG)

The young root of a tropical plant which is indispensable in all types of oriental cookery. If the ginger is fresh, the skin can easily be scraped off; otherwise peel with a sharp knife. Ginger can be used in every dish if your taste is so inclined. It is usual to cut off a small length of 2.5 cm (1 in) and then mince or crush it according to the recipe. When ginger is preserved in sweet syrup it is usually used for dessert, but if green ginger is unavailable, wash off the syrup, then slice the ginger and add it to your dish. Using ginger powder will not give the same effect, but will impart a gingery taste to the food.

Glutinous rice flour

糯米粉 (NOR MEI FUN)

This flour is extracted from glutinous rice, also known as 'sticky' rice. The grains are small and white. Glutinous rice can also be cooked and used in dishes which call for ordinary rice. (It is best to soak it for at least 1 hour before cooking.) The flour is extensively used in making desserts and can be used instead of cornflour for thickening.

Hoisin sauce

海鮮醬 (HOISIN JEUNG)

This dark brown, sweet sauce is obtainable in cans or jars. It is made from soy beans, sugar, spices, hot chillies, garlic and ginger root. It is known as Chinese barbecue sauce and is also used as a dip. The pancakes eaten with Peking Duck are spread with it. When making roast pork or spare ribs or anything that needs to be barbecued, use hoisin sauce in the marinade. The sauce needs to be taken out of the can and stored in a glass or china jar in the refrigerator, and will keep indefinitely.

Lemon grass jelly
涼粉 (LOONG FUN)

This is available in cans and is made from the essence of lemon grass and agar-agar. It is a darkish green jelly which makes an attractive colour combination with different flavoured ice creams. It is very refreshing served chilled on its own.

Lime water
宜母子汁 (YIN MO CHI JUP)

Fresh lime juice with water added to dilute.

Mirin
料酒 (LIU JO)

This is a sweet rice wine which is used only for cooking. It is also known as a second-grade *sake*, which is Japanese rice wine. if necessary, substitute with a sweet sherry.

Oyster sauce
蠔油 (HOR YO)

There is an oyster sauce and oyster essence available. Oyster sauce is made from fresh oysters, soy sauce, spices and seasonings and when added to other foods while cooking imparts a rich flavour. It is unique in flavour and texture and so there is no substitute that would be satisfactory. It comes in bottles and cans, and will keep indefinitely if stored in a cool place.

Pork caul

網油 (MUNG YO)

This very fine white net-like fat is purchased from Chinese delicatessens in sheets. It is wrapped around the food, and when deep-fried, the fat dissolves into the food and produces a very fine crisp coating. Part of the lesser omentum of the pig (see also caul fat).

Preserved eggs

皮蛋 (PEE DARN)

These are known as 'hundred-year-old eggs' but in reality are only preserved for a hundred days. They are duck eggs which are covered with black lime and rice husks. When they are ready, the black lime is peeled off and they are shelled and washed. The outside is gelatinous and a greeny colour and the yolk is the colour of blue cheese. The eggs are sliced and served with ginger pickles,

Preserved salted vegetable

葱菜 (CHOONG CHOY)

This vegetable is available in packets, jars or cans. It is actually a large turnip which is preserved with salt and spices. It is salty and crisp, and adds an exotic flavour to pork and beef dishes. This vegetable is also used to flavour rice soup (*jook*) and noodles, minced finely and sprinkled on top.

Preserved green vegetable

冬菜 (DOONG CHOY)

This preserved vegetable is usually obtained in squat deep brown earthenware jars and keeps indefinitely in the refrigerator. The fresh vegetable has a hard bulb from which grows a green stem and every part of the vegetable is used in the preserving process. It is particularly good when combined with pork and is used in the classic Cantonese dish of steamed pork, *Ko yuk* (a winter dish); it is also used to accompany rice flour noodles.

Red dates

紅棗 (HOONG JOH)

These are a variety of Chinese dates which have red skins and dark brown flesh. They must be soaked in warm water for 10 minutes and washed before use. If they are used in soup, just wash them first, then add. These were once inexpensive, but are now a luxury item on the shopping list.

Rice wine

米酒 (MEI JO)

There are various rice wines, and a recipe for one type has been included on page 75 so you can make some yourself. Rice wine gives an exotic flavour to food unlike any substitute you may use, but a sweet sherry is the closest. When drinking rice wine, it is warmed first and then drunk out of small wine cups.

Rose petal sugar

豆蓉 (DOW YUNG)

This sugar is used in Moon cakes (see p.63). It is made by packing red rose petals in sugar and leaving for 9 to 12 months to allow oil from petals to permeate sugar.

Salted duck eggs

鹹蛋 (HARM DARN)

These eggs are preserved with brine and when ready to be used must be boiled. The whites are very salty and the yolks are a brilliant orange colour. They may also be cooked in the rice during the final stages of cooking. See recipe, page 44.

Shirataki

日本粉條

These are clear Japanese noodles made from the yam plant. They are obtainable in cans and in packets already par-boiled and in their own liquor. They are more expensive than cellophane noodles, which are an excellent substitute, but their texture is more elastic.

Water chestnuts

馬蹄 (MAR TAY)

This annual waterplant with fruits like a tiny buffalo head is native to China and is also cultivated in Japan and Taiwan. It can also be

grown anywhere wet rice is cultivated, because it can be planted between the rows of rice in the first stage when the water is necessary to the young rice plants. When the black-brown skin is peeled away it reveals a creamy white crisp fruit which is used in various dishes.
Water chestnuts are available in cans and are also preserved in honey, and candied. There is no comparison in taste and sweetness to the fresh product, but if fresh ones are unobtainable, canned ones are a good substitute. The seeds of the plant can also be made into powder and used for thickening.

Wheat starch flour

糖麵粉 (DUNG MIN FUN)

This is pure wheat flour. It is available only at oriental delicatessens, in 454 g (1 lb) packets. It is used in the making of *har gow* and other dumplings, and produces a transparent pastry.

Index

Numbers in bold type indicate the page on which the recipe occurs

INDEX

INDEX

INDEX